March 3, 2001

Dear Rob and Pam,

May God bless you two in your life's journey, and thank you for your hospitality!

+ Eugene Sutton

The Diversity of Centering Prayer

D016681?

The Diversity of
Centering Prayer

Edited by Gustave Reininger

CONTINUUM • NEW YORK

1999

The Continuum Publishing Company
370 Lexington Avenue
New York, NY 10017

Copyright © 1999 by Gustave Reininger
"The Method of Centering Prayer" by Thomas Keating © 1995
St. Benedict's Monastery

Cynthia Bourgeault's "Centering Prayer as Radical Consent"
was originally published in *Sewanee Theological Review* 40:1
(Christmas/December 1996), published quarterly by The School
of Theology of The University of the South in Sewanee, Tennessee.

All rights reserved.
No part of this book may be reproduced,
stored in a retrieval system, or transmitted,
in any form or by any means,
electronic, mechanical, photocopying,
recording, or otherwise,
without the written permission of
The Continuum Publishing Company.

Printed in the United States of America

Library of Congress Cataloging-in-Publication Data

The diversity of centering prayer / edited by Gustave Reininger.
     p.   cm.
  Includes bibliographical references.
  ISBN 0-8264-1115-0 (pbk.)
  1. Contemplation. I. Reininger, Gustave.
BV5091.C7D58 1999
248.3'4—dc21   99-18005
                                      CIP

CONTENTS

Preface ✿

GUSTAVE REININGER

This collection, along with its companion volume, *Centering Prayer in Daily Life and Ministry,* emerged from the Centering Prayer Program at the Parish of St. Matthew in Pacific Palisades, California, and from the generous support for this program by Trinity Episcopal Church of Wall Street, New York. From the many who have benefited from the program, deep gratitude is due St. Matthew's Rector, the Rev. David Walton Miller; Gale Reininger, the program's director; Fr. Thomas Keating; and the Rev. James G. Callaway and Dr. Robert Carle of Trinity Episcopal Church. Also great thanks is extended to Gene Gollogly of the Continuum Publishing Group, who has shown great vision as a publisher to become a significant supporter of today's renewal of the contemplative dimension of spirituality.

The Diversity of Centering Prayer contains many challenging insights and experiences of the fruits of a regular practice of Centering Prayer. Its ecumenical list of contributors points up the broad appeal of Centering Prayer as a common ground of Christian unity. The topic of diversity is meant to demonstrate the broad range of experience and insight into the practice and conceptual background of Centering Prayer within the Christian contemplative tradition. In a collaboration between lay spirituality and the ancient monastic traditions, Centering Prayer has evolved into a living testament to Thomas Merton's call for the contemplative dimension in an active life.

This volume is also intended as a modest proposal, perhaps a challenge, to those who already practice and share Centering Prayer to write of their experience and insight. There are many significant voices beyond the founders of the spiritual network of those practicing Centering Prayer. Their contribution to the growing literature on Centering Prayer would be invaluable in helping Centering Prayer take lasting root in today's spirituality.

Fr. M. Basil Pennington's essay, "A Living Tradition," places Centering Prayer within the contemplative lineages of both the Western and Eastern Christian tradition. Fr. Pennington reminds us that methods of prayer are hallowed and prevalent in the Christian contemplative tradition, dating back to the Desert Fathers and Mothers. Centering Prayer, though a recent development, draws its inspiration and methodology from this ancient tradition.

Fr. Thomas Keating's offering, "Practicing Centering Prayer," is perhaps his most concise, yet encompassing, statement of the method and conceptual background of Centering Prayer. It is a distillation of many years of teaching and reflecting on the experience of those practicing Centering Prayer on a regular daily basis. It addresses both the newcomer and the experienced with a discussion of the prayer practice and the central issues of growth on the contemplative path.

Carmelite theologian and teacher, Ernest Larkin of Catholic University, compares and contrasts Centering Prayer and Dom John Main's method of Christian Meditation as new, yet traditionally derived, methods of leading to contemplative prayer. As a Carmelite, Fr. Larkin examines the links of these new approaches to the traditional contributions of St. John of the Cross and St. Teresa of Avila. Fr. Larkin's shares his insights into how the contemplative currents of Christianity continue to evolve, responsive to both today's spiritual needs and to the unchanging nature of contemplative prayer.

The Rev. Cynthia Bourgeault, a hermit-priest in the Episcopalian Church, offers a very stimulating and singular analysis of "Centering Prayer as Radical Consent." From a perspective of willingness and willfulness, she draws on the work of Gerald May to frame Centering Prayer as an exercise of intention rather than attention or focusing—a deeply receptive prayer form that opens us to God's presence and action within us. In doing so, she makes significant connections between Centering Prayer, psychology, and theology. Cynthia's is a voice that deserves to be encouraged and nurtured for its thoughtful insight and instruction.

Fr. Eugene Sutton of St. Columba's Episcopal Church shares his perspectives on the contemplative dimensions of African-American Spirituality. His rich essay on the central concepts and significant voices in the African-American contemplative tradition suggests enormous promise for teaching Centering Prayer beyond its predominantly middle class, middle-aged Anglo constituency.

Centering Prayer groups as small communities is the subject of Lyla Yastion's study of actual Centering Prayer groups in New York, "Where Two or Three Are Gathered." Unvarnished observations confirm that the delicate experience of Contemplative Prayer in daily life is best nurtured and developed through a small group support structure. Studying actual groups at various levels of participation and development, Dr. Yastion balances the observation of a social scientist and the insights of a practitioner and teacher of Centering Prayer.

Kay Lindahl, a lay teacher in the Episcopal Church, offers a powerful and practical piece on "Centering Prayer and the Art of Dialogue." It constitutes almost an instruction manual for conducting Centering Prayer small group dialogue. Her concrete, practical guidelines on how to keep the shared exchanges within the realm of dialogue can be of great help in avoiding the risk of groups becoming a forum for theological, therapeutical, or philosophical debate. Kay's observations, which draw deeply on the work of physicist David Bohm, discuss the significant reality that through dialogue we can consent to God's presence and action within the group, just as we consent within our individual hearts during Centering Prayer.

"Introducing Centering Prayer into the Curriculum at an Ecumenical Seminary" is a distillation of Dr. George Cairns's experience teaching Centering Prayer at the Chicago Theological Seminary. Dr. Cairns relates how he went about teaching Centering Prayer in a challenging intellectual environment, questioning the prevailing view in seminary communities that contemplation is otherworldly and impractical.

The final offering, "Forgiving the Unforgivable," was written by Fr. Basil Pennington in Pacific Palisades, California, during a stopover on his way home to Spencer Abbey to retire. Fr. Basil had just concluded a nine-year residency at Our Lady of Joy, the Trappist Monastery on Lantau, Hong Kong. While there, he helped revitalize the monastic community and traveled widely in China and Asia on missions for both the Roman Catholic Church and the Trappist order, as well as his own ministry of sharing Centering Prayer. Fr. Basil had come to California by way of a harrowing trip to East Africa where he had been invited to teach Centering Prayer and *lectio divina*. Instead of holding workshops, he had a first hand encounter with some of the most barbaric evil in our world today. Resting here in California, between praying, working on his Internet ministries, and daily rounds of swimming, Fr. Basil struggled to reconcile the stark spiritual contradictions of his trip to East Africa. His essay shares his practical realization that even the most harrowing of human atrocity bends its knee in the presence of God. As we took Fr. Basil to his plane, his joviality reawakened. He looked out at the Pacific Ocean and laughed heartily, noting that Thomas Merton also stopped off in California before his retirement.

Gustave Reininger
Pacific Palisades, California

1 ❀

Centering Prayer: A Living Tradition

M. Basil Pennington

How did Jesus pray when he spent those nights in prayer?

The disciples asked him. But we do not find his response in the Gospels. There are simple directives about prayer found here and there in the written accounts, but for the rest we depend on the oral tradition. John has assured us that it is abundant, ending his written account with the statement that not all the books in the world could get it all down.

Early in the tradition, in the very first centuries, we find the Fathers, the earliest teachers of contemplative prayer, speaking of the *mono logion,* the "one word" prayer. This tradition was first brought to the west by the young seeker John Cassian, who learned it at the end of the fourth century from Abba Isaac. This venerable ancient told John it was what he learned when he was a young man, and he added that he too had learned it from a venerable ancient. The living tradition was being passed on.

To understand more easily the teaching Abba Isaac gave John, we need to be in touch with the practice still alive among our Byzantine brothers and sisters. Today, if a young, or not so young, man or woman decides to pursue their life in Christ more seriously, they will go in quest of a spiritual father or mother. The seeker will ask the pneumaticos: "Father/Mother, give me a word for prayer." The spiritual guide will give the disciple a word from Scripture. A very common one, actually a double word, was taken from two different Gospel stories: "Lord, Jesus Christ, Son of the living God, have mercy on me a sinner." At the same time, the guide will give the disciple a prayer cord with some fifty or one hundred knots, with directions to say the prayer so many times, using the cord. After some time, the disciple will return and report to the spiritual father/mother the thoughts that have come up as he or she said the prayer. In the light of this manifestation of thoughts, the guide will alter the prayer formula. Gradually, it will be simplified until it becomes the simple word: Jesus. And thus, we have the Jesus Prayer in its purest and simplest form.

But the word Abba Isaac gave John Cassian was not this most common one but rather the first sentence of Psalm 69: "O God, come to my assistance. O Lord, make haste to help me." As the spiritual guide in the west led the disciple to the simplicity of one word, it did not come in practice to one common word. Rather, it kept a certain flexibility. So the author of *The Cloud of Unknowing* put it this way: "Choose a word, a simple word, a single syllable word is best, like God or love, but choose a word that is meaningful to you."

But this brings us into a later period of the living tradition. Earlier, among the more educated monks of the West, prayer did not remain so dependent on a guide. The monk or nun sat with her text of the Scriptures, listening to the Lord speaking through the inspired word. The reader-listener would allow a word to emerge from the text and let it resonate within, expanding consciousness to a more godlike sense of perception and bringing the mind down into the heart, where it evoked a response and led gently into the center, where one rested in love.

However, the leisure that allowed the monk or nun to sit long in this contemplative process was a luxury not enjoyed by many. Moreover, with the development of the schools, a more rationalist approach toward *lectio divina* began to prevail, an approach that did not lend itself readily to the openness of contemplation, but rather to more rational discourse and the use of images. Thus, *lectio* and contemplation became somewhat detached. The author of *The Cloud of Unknowing* guides his son in a way of contemplative prayer that while not immediately attached to his own *lectio,* was grounded in a *lectio* that enlivened the faith and love necessary to make the word a meaningful expression of faith and love. This separation or division seems to better serve people today whose lives are filled with many activities. It is more possible for those with many business and family obligations to carve out a couple of twenty-minute periods and perhaps another ten for *lectio* than to find an hour or two of continuous free time for contemplative leisure.

While the practice continued serenely in many parts of Eastern Christendom, in others the deep spirituality of Islamic conquerors came to have influence. Thus, there developed some highly psychosomatic methods of praying the Jesus Prayer. For the most part, these did not make their way to the West. Rather what happened in the West was an almost total eclipse of the practice. This was due in part to the loss of the teachers of the prayer with the destruction of the monasteries. But it was also fostered by a defensive hierarchy, which came to fear what it could not readily submit to its more rationalist examination.

The mighty flow of the Spirit in the midst of our century called forth a renewal of the contemplative dimension in the life of all Christians. In response to this and, we hope, under the influence of the Spirit, the way of Centering Prayer emerged and spread to many parts of the Church.

It is a living tradition, and thus, as it has been received by different teachers, it has been differently shaped. Fr. Thomas Keating after some years of teaching settled upon "Four Guidelines." I have usually offered the prayer in three simple rules or points. Fr. John Main, somewhat in the spirit of the early Church, which borrowed freely from the prevailing pagan practices, brought in from his experience among Hindus the use of a mantra. This introduction does quite significantly alter the approach to the prayer. It becomes a prayer more concerned with attention and less purely upon intention. Because of this difference, two movements have developed, reaching out across the globe: the Christian Meditation Movement promoting the method developed by Fr. John Main and the Contemplative Outreach sharing Centering Prayer around the world.

The differences reflect undoubtedly the differences of the teachers. As we just mentioned, John's experience with a Hindu master shaped his later practice of the prayer of Saint John Cassian. Fr. Thomas, a monk of powerful intellect and clarity of mind as well as a rich background in mystical study, offers a carefully nuanced teaching. My own is more simple, flowing more directly from the Gospel teaching of our Lord.

But the prayer presentation is not only formed by the teacher, but also by a sensitivity to the recipients. In Dominica, I was told there could not be any kind of gathering without singing, so the teaching and meditation session were preceded and followed by song. Indeed, while we meditated, we could hear the pounding of dancing feet from above and the pounding of drums from the surrounding streets. Who says you need quiet to meditate? In South Africa, the openness for Christian meditation was prepared by yoga—many like to do a bit of stretching before the meditation, but one has to be cautious about these add-ons. There was a booklet produced in Kashmir which said it was better to meditate once a day for an hour rather than twice a day. But this little booklet had added on so many things that it took a good half-hour to get into the meditation. Posture, too, is something that differs much with the culture. Asiatics often settle comfortably in postures that would be anything but restful for us from the West.

I have been impressed how the simple presentation of the method, keeping close to the Gospels, has found a receptive audience in many diverse cultures. The simplicity is much appreciated. Peoples from diverse religious traditions seem to be able to get the point of the Gospel stories, though when speaking of God sometimes it has been better to speak of the Divine Spirit within or the Higher Power.

I have spoken of only three of the present-day teachers. This is certainly not because there are not others, but because these three have been looked to as leaders. Fr. William Meniger was very active in the early renewal of this way of prayer, and the teaching of Fr. John Main has been ably carried forward by his disciple, Fr. Laurence Freeman. Fr. Giles Cong has been bringing the prayer to the seminaries of China. And a Jesuit, Fr. Thomas Clark, has written beautifully of it. There is a great desire on the part of all of these to do all they can to foster an emerging lay leadership which has already proved its capability as teachers and bearers of the tradition, especially in the Philippines, South Africa, and Malaysia.

The name itself, Centering Prayer, is new in the tradition. The author of *The Cloud of Unknowing* does use the term but more in an active sense: "Center all your attention and desire on him. . . ."

The Prayer has had diverse names through the centuries, and these same names have had diverse meanings. Thomas Merton, Fr. Louis of Gethsemani, inspired this new name, but it was first formulated by a La Salette father. It was not copyrighted and soon became quite popular. Then it was applied to different forms of prayer. Fr. Earnest Larkin produced a set of tapes featuring three kinds of Centering Prayer. One was very much St. Theresa of Jesus' imaginative prayer; another, St. Ignatius's prayer of discernment; and the third, a sort of mix of the methods of Fr. John Main and Centering Prayer. Today, after twenty-five years of teaching and experience, there is perhaps a greater precision in identifying Centering Prayer as the prayer of *The Cloud of Unknowing* and of St. John Cassian.

The tradition moves on, healthy, strong, and very much alive as it makes its way into the twenty-first century and the new millenium. What it will be called, who will be teaching it, and just how it will be packaged in 2999—no one knows, but as long as the Christian community is true to its heritage, this way of prayer will be made known. For it is the Prayer of the Heart, prayer in the heart. It is at the heart of the Christian experience, an authentically ancient Christian way of opening to the joy, peace, and fulfillment of contemplation.

2 ✸

Practicing Centering Prayer

THOMAS KEATING

St. Teresa of Ávila once wrote that all difficulties in prayer come from one single flaw: *praying as if God were absent*. Many of our difficulties in daily life are probably the result of *living as if God were absent*. The impression is sometimes given in religious instruction that God is outside of us. On the contrary, God is totally present to us all the time: closer than thinking, closer than breathing, closer than choosing, closer than consciousness itself. God could not be any closer. God is so close that, in a sense, he is our true self.

The chief wound of the human condition is the monumental illusion that God is absent. We have self-consciousness, but without the experience of union with God, self-reflection often gives rise to feelings of fear, guilt, and acute loneliness. Because the human heart is designed for limitless happiness, truth, and love, nothing less than that kind of fulfillment can satisfy our innate longing.

Because we all come into this world in a state of complete helplessness, even the neutral events of early life may be interpreted as traumatic or painful. As a result, we may experience an increasing sense of alienation and aloneness in what we perceive to be an unsafe world. We try to defend ourselves from

these painful feelings by developing complex emotional programs that search for happiness in symbols of security, esteem,
and power provided by the culture or environment in which we
are raised. The aggregate of compensatory programs for the pain
of our emotional wounds together with our over-identification
with cultural values might be called the false self. It is the
source of all our ordinary thoughts and feelings. It is who we
think we are.

Contemplative prayer, of which Centering Prayer is a first
step, is a kind of divine psychotherapy that dismantles the false
self system. It heals the emotional wounds of a lifetime and opens
us to the possibility of experiencing intimacy with God, even
Divine union.

In Centering Prayer, we sit in silence for twenty or thirty
minutes and open to the spiritual level of our awareness by disregarding the thoughts, feelings, and impressions on the surface
of our consciousness. A word of one or two syllables such as God,
Abba, or Jesus, serves to maintain or renew our intention. The
Christian contemplative tradition recommends a discipline of
prayer that enables us to disengage temporarily from our usual
flow of thoughts. Our ordinary thoughts tend to reflect the mind-
sets, prepackaged values, and preconceived ideas that we learned
in childhood. To stop thinking about them for twenty minutes is
like taking a much-needed vacation.

When we begin to pray in this way, we observe that our consciousness is like a river that is constantly flowing. On the surface
are all kinds of particular ideas, memories, sense perceptions, and
emotions that we might compare to boats. Indeed, we are so
dominated by the awareness of boats that we rarely see the river
itself on which the boats are floating. Beneath the surface of this
river of consciousness is the Divine Indwelling, the God who is
the source of our being at every level: body, soul, and spirit. In
Centering Prayer, we consent to God's presence and to receive
Divine love without self-reflection. We move beyond thoughts
and feelings into a more intimate exchange with God, from conversation to communion. Thus, Meister Eckhart calls contemplation the "unknowing knowing of God."

The purpose of Centering Prayer is not self-perfection or self-preoccupation, but to move beyond ourselves into God. We turn ourselves over completely to God and consent to God's presence at the deepest level of our being. To be able to hear God fully, we have to learn the discipline of interior silence. St. John of the Cross says, "The Father spoke from all eternity just one Word. He spoke it in an eternal silence and it is in silence that we hear It." This is a magnificent summary of what we do in contemplative prayer. It is also the ultimate healing.

There are four basic guidelines for practicing Centering Prayer. The first guideline is to choose a sacred word of one or two syllables as the symbol of our intention to open and yield to God's presence and action within us. A visual analogy, such as being under God's loving gaze or of turning toward God inwardly as if to look at someone you love, may also be used. One does not visualize a specific image.

It is recommended to take a moment of silence to choose a particular word that would be suitable for you. It could be one of the holy names of God, and this is preferred, but it could also be some other kind of word. For instance, if you harbor negative ideas of God for one reason or another, using a particular name of God might not be advisable because when the thought of God arises, your negative feelings might surface and prevent you from quieting down. Other more general words, such as *love, peace, shalom, calm, oneness, stillness, mercy, faith, praise,* or *presence,* might be more comfortable than specifically religious terms. In any case, don't be anxious about choosing a word. It is not the meaning of the word that is important, but rather the fact that it manifests your intention to consent to God's presence and action within you. When choosing the sacred word, it is recommended that you close your eyes for a moment and turn inwardly, opening to the presence of the Holy Spirit, and ask for a word that might be especially useful. If you are not sure, just choose one that comes to mind so that you can at least experiment with that one.

It is important not to change the word during the time of prayer because the process of choosing another word is itself fraught with thinking particular thoughts. One purpose of this prayer is to learn to let go of particular thoughts during the period of prayer. The next time you do this, you could try another word if you wish, but the sooner you settle on one the better. If you decide to pursue this practice of Centering Prayer, the word that you use regularly during the prayer period tends to be sown in the subconscious so that it becomes second nature to say it. It rises up during prayer and comes to your assistance when you are beginning to think other thoughts.

The second guideline is sit comfortably with your eyes closed and settle briefly. Choose a position that you will not have to change during the twenty-minute period of prayer; when the body is still, the mind also tends to be quiet. Most people choose to sit in a chair with their feet on the floor and their back relatively straight. The principle is to choose a position in which for twenty minutes you will not experience discomfort, because that would be a thought, a perception, and we are trying to leave behind all particular perceptions. Lying down or using a headrest are both not recommended because the body tends to associate these postures with sleep.

Having settled comfortably and closed our eyes and begun letting go of our surroundings and of our interior preoccupations, we silently introduce our sacred word as the symbol of our consent to God's presence and action within us. We do this with our minds, not vocally with our lips or voice. We repeat it slowly, without trying to articulate it carefully. We let it say itself, so to speak. It may become vague or even disappear briefly. In the beginning we normally have to say the sacred word almost constantly. After the process becomes well established, we need only return to it in order to reaffirm our consent to God's presence when it gets challenged by some attractive thought that is going down the stream of consciousness.

It is hard to find a place in most homes today where you can encounter silence. Try to choose a time and place where you can sit for twenty minutes without being disturbed by an interruption like a phone ringing or someone trying to talk to you. At times during prayer, you may be withdrawn from the external senses to some degree. Out of respect for them, it is a good idea to avoid being jarred out of Centering Prayer too suddenly.

The first few times you practice Centering Prayer, you might actually fall asleep. And that is fine. If you are doing the prayer correctly, you are assuming a receptive attitude. That may mean that for the first time in recent weeks or months you are giving the body a chance to relax. Many people repress how tired they are because they have so much to do. As a result, when they sit down and relax during this prayer, the body calls for what it needs. So don't be surprised if you should drop off. When you wake up, start where you left off. Don't feel bad about the time spent in physical rest. Still, it is a good idea to choose a time when you are most alert, so that you don't doze your way through these precious moments. If you do feel drowsy the first few times, it will gradually subside.

The third and the most important guideline is that when we become aware of thoughts, we return ever so gently to the sacred word. Whenever we notice a thought, feeling, impression, memory, or external stimulus that attracts our attention, we gently return to the sacred word as a way of reaffirming our original intention to consent to God's presence and action within us.

The sacred word is not intended to overpower or force thoughts away. The sacred word is not a baseball bat to knock thoughts and feelings out of the ballpark, nor is it a bulldozer to clear thoughts out of our way. Rather, it is the interior discipline of *disregarding* thoughts by turning our attention to the Divine presence within. Given the fact that we are creatures in time, everything that comes down the stream of consciousness will emerge into the foreground and then disappear downstream. We take a friendly attitude towards thoughts. We resist no thought, retain no thought, and react emotionally to no thought and return to the sacred word when we notice we are thinking some other thought. If we have expectations of having no thoughts at all, we might feel that we are not doing the prayer correctly. Thoughts are a normal part of the process of Centering Prayer because our imagination is a perpetual motion faculty and is always grinding out some image or reflection. The essence of Centering Prayer is opening and consenting to the presence of God in faith. Our discipline is to let thoughts and perceptions enter our awareness and let them pass by returning ever so gently to the sacred word, the symbol of God's presence within us.

We begin by silently introducing our sacred word and saying it slowly and without effort: just thinking it, which is a very easy kind of activity. Little by little, we may begin to feel attracted to interior silence, peace, and refreshment. When thoughts come down the stream of consciousness and pull us back to the surface of our ordinary thinking, we ever so gently return to the sacred word.

Our awareness during Centering Prayer is something like a balloon floating up and down in the breeze. When the wind is becalmed, the balloon slowly sinks to the earth, the symbol of peace, refreshment, and quiet. Then, just as we are about to enter into what seems like a delightful space, a little zephyr (a thought) comes from nowhere and pushes our awareness back to thinking once again

This going down and up may seem disconcerting at first, as though nothing is being accomplished. But a growing habit of consenting to God's presence and action within us is gradually being established. This consent opens us to the Divine light, life, and love. By turning our general loving attention to this deeper level, we let go of the fascination and domination of particular thoughts, memories, feelings, impressions, and perceptions and cultivate a general loving attentiveness to God.

Centering Prayer can be difficult if you identify prayer primarily as thoughts expressed in words. Verbal prayer is one expression of prayer but not the only expression. In Centering Prayer, we open ourselves to God without commentaries that may accompany verbal prayer, however devout these might be. Evagrius, one of the Desert Fathers, defines prayer as "the laying aside of thoughts."

This does not mean that we do not pray with words and even converse with God at other times. In fact, other forms of prayer will be energized, invigorated, and given a depth that they did not have before. The capacity just to be with God begins to grow, filling us every now and then in daily life with the sense of God's presence. The goal of contemplative prayer is to be continually in contact with God's presence within, so that it becomes a kind of fourth dimension to our three-dimensional space-time world. Rooted in this inner experience of the Divine Presence, we begin to penetrate outward appearances and to perceive the Divine Presence at the deepest levels of everyone and everything that we encounter.

The first few times people do Centering Prayer, they often complain, "I didn't feel anything. I didn't get any good out of it." But this is an emotional judgment coming from the false self. It is based on the way we make most of our judgments: did it feel good or didn't it? If it didn't *feel* good, we think it must not have *been* good. But this is completely unreliable because we are using our emotional faculties to judge something that is on the spiritual plane. We have to do this prayer with great simplicity, without expectations about what might happen.

The fourth guideline is that after practicing Centering Prayer for twenty or thirty minutes, we take a little time to return to the ordinary awareness of the external senses and the usual flow of thoughts. We do this by keeping our eyes closed for a couple of minutes and beginning to think in our usual way. A vocal prayer may be helpful at this time. This brief transition may bring some of the peace that we have experienced during our prayer time into our ordinary lives.

Another complaint that many people make in their first few months of Centering Prayer is that they have so many thoughts that they think they were better off when they were doing some other kind of prayer. When we experience thoughts throughout the whole time of Centering Prayer, without any experience of interior refreshment or peace, this does not prove that it is not having an effect on us. The power of the Divine light works on a level that is not accessible to any of our ordinary faculties. If we are waiting upon God, consenting to God's presence by continually returning to the sacred word, even if we are not successful in letting go of the thoughts that come by, then little by little, we will be free from our ordinary flow of thoughts and experience a spiritual attentiveness.

This experience of spiritual attentiveness is characterized by no reflection of self. The knower, the knowing, and that which is known are all one. Awareness alone remains. It is the infusion of love and knowledge together, and while it is going on, it is non-reflective. This is sometimes called "resting in God." You don't know about it until you emerge from it. In the beginning, it is so tenuous that you may think you were asleep. The experience is temporary, but it orients us toward the contemplative state.

Sometimes our psychological experience is that there are so many thoughts, so much inner noise, that we cannot pray at all. But that is not true. As long as we choose to remain in this inner sanctuary, that is where we actually are. In fact, thoughts cannot touch us there because we are not on a level where distractions take place, which is in our imagination, memory, and reasoning powers. Our prayer continues because that is our intention. The bombardment of thoughts is one of those things with which we just put up. Experience shows that once the psyche has adapted to this way of relating to God in a receptive mode, thoughts gradually begin to thin out.

However, once in a while, there are so many thoughts and emotions on our inner stream of consciousness that we feel over-whelmed and cannot even find our sacred word. It is like being in a hurricane or typhoon, and our sacred word, like a buoy, is buried under the waves. If we cannot do anything except be battered by the turmoil, we *allow the situation itself* to be the sacred symbol of opening and consenting to God's presence and action within us. In this way, we do not fight the bombardment of thoughts or react emotionally by saying, "This is awful! I used to pray better when I used words!" or any other emotional judgment based on the psychological content of a particular period of prayer.

Over a long period of time, the depths of the unconscious are healed by the practice of Centering Prayer. Just as the body has its natural means of evacuating toxic waste and moving to health, the psyche has the capacity to evacuate the psycho-toxins arising from the emotionally undigested material of early child-hood. When the rest in prayer is deep, the defense mechanisms that keep these emotional blocks in place start to loosen up. The psyche then releases them using our awareness during the time of Centering Prayer as the channel of evacuation.

No two periods of Centering Prayer can be expected to be the same. While we might experience deep rest in one period of prayer, we may experience just the opposite in the next. The reason often is that we may have accessed such deep rest in the first period that we have loosened up the hardpan around certain emotional blocks, and the unloading process begins. This material appears in our awareness as a jumble of emotionally charged thoughts and even primitive feelings.

To get a better sense of this purging process, suppose that we are starting our Centering Prayer period with our sacred word. We open to the Divine Indwelling at the root of our being. As the sacred word is gently repeated, we enter a state of interior rest because we are not thinking our usual thoughts or enduring our usual reactions to them. In the measure that this rest is deep and brings comfort, we loosen up the emotional material in the unconscious. The rest also relaxes places in the body where stress and tension have been stored. It is widely held that the mind and body are not separate but integrated, and that all of the negative experiences from childhood are stored in our nervous system and in the tissues of our body. The refreshment of prayer acts on the physical as well as the spiritual level.

It is important to remember that the psyche may occasionally use our awareness during Centering Prayer as a channel of evacuation. The distress we experience might be described as a kind of psychic nausea. We need to let distressing emotions come to awareness and not push them back into our psychological stomach so to speak, where they will continue to cause indigestion. We just let everything go by. Since it is on the way out, we do not have to do anything with it except endure it. During this process, we may experience primitive emotions which we repressed in order to survive at an early stage of life. Instead of fearing or lamenting their escape, we would do better to rejoice and wave a cheerful good-bye.

Since these repressed thoughts and emotions come from past experiences and are well buried in our unconscious, they might seem to the conscious mind as if they are coming from an unknown source. The conscious mind, accustomed to having a recent cause or stimulus for such raw feelings—su ch as a recent unpleasant experience—may become uneasy not perceiving the source of these strong emotions. You may say to yourself, "This is horrible. I never felt panic like this before (or this raw anger or depression). I was a good person. Everybody thought I was a model in the community. And I thought so too, and here I am having these primitive emotions! There must be something wrong!" But if we wait out the unloading process, this emotional junk will gradually dissipate along with the confusion that it created in our mind and the disruption it might have caused in our relationships with others.

Centering Prayer is not psychotherapy. It is not a question of analyzing or discovering what the original difficulty was that might have caused the emotional damage. It is simply a process of unloading the emotional garbage of a lifetime. When we empty the garbage, most of us don't separate the eggshells from the banana peels. We just throw the whole thing into the dumpster.

Once in a while, something might come up during this practice of Centering Prayer that may require some spiritual counseling by a psychologically trained person. However, normally, if we can put up with the purging process, it heals our deepest wounds and uncovers the Divine presence that was present within us all along.

Carl Jung, the noted psychiatrist, taught that every person has a repressed side to their personality, the shadow, which we dislike or disown, either because of our own prejudices or because it is unacceptable in society. Accordingly, most persons do not want to look at their dark side. It is so painful to recognize and acknowledge that we often project it onto other people where we can continue to despise it in them. Obviously, this is an enormous obstacle to relating with a person on whom we are projecting. We cannot minister to that person or even hear his or her needs because everything is first filtered through our own emotional investment in disliking them so we do not have to dislike ourselves. This is a normal dynamic, and we do not have to be ashamed of it. However, we should be aware of it and take steps to heal it. One of the greatest advances in our spiritual growth is to submit to the purification of the Spirit leading to liberation from our false self. This is what the fullness of redemption really is, the redemption from the false self and from the obstacles that it places to Divine union.

In order to enjoy the free flow of grace and to relate to others as they are, this process of purification is one of the highest priorities when we give ourselves to the following of Christ. It is not enough just to desire Divine union. We must take the appropriate steps to reduce the obstacles to its unfolding. The Christian contemplative tradition has provided us with various disciplines that prepare us for contemplative prayer. Centering Prayer is a contemporary expression of this tradition.

We recommend doing two twenty to thirty minute periods of prayer each day. This may seem like a considerable commitment and, to some people, almost impossible. But if they make the sacrifices to do it, they may be happily surprised. If you commit yourself to practicing Centering Prayer for a reasonable length of time (such as three months), you will know by that time whether it really fits you.

Doing Centering Prayer as a regular practice helps us to recognize that God is always present. We experience that rest and activity can be united in a mysterious oneness when the love of God is the source of both our activity and our prayer. After Centering Prayer has gradually dismantled the false self system, we will experience Divine union as an abiding state.

3 ✸

Contemplative Prayer Forms Today: Are They Contemplation?

Ernest E. Larkin

A simpler title could be: "Contemplative Prayer Today and Contemplation: Are They the Same or Different?" And if different, what is their content and how are they related? This paper attempts a clarification of terms.

But it is not just a question of semantics. We are asking what we are doing when we are practicing contemporary forms of contemplative prayer, such as Centering Prayer or the "Christian Meditation" of John Main. Are we praying actively, calling on our human resources under the impulse of grace, or are we submitting passively to some presumed heightened action of God within us, perhaps experiencing infused contemplation that is too subtle to recognize? Do these prayer forms presume we have reached a state of contemplation beyond the level of ordinary meditation? Or may anyone, beginner or experienced, take them up? Or, bluntly, could our silence and quietude, our disengagement from the work of the imagination or intellect in the prayer, be an exercise of woolgathering, daydreaming, spinning our wheels, and thus wasting time by willful inactivity? Worse still, could we be falling into the error of quietism, cultivating idleness and passivity, with nothing going on inside? This error gave contemplative prayer a bad name from the seventeenth century to the beginning of the twentieth. It is an error that could crop up again today.

What do we mean by contemplative prayer and contemplation? For most writers the two terms are interchangeable, and their content runs the gamut of mental prayer, from ordinary meditation to infused contemplation. John Main, the architect of Christian Meditation, begins a series of talks with the statement: "I am using the term meditation as synonymous to contemplation, contemplative prayer, meditative prayer, and so forth."[1] Sometimes the two terms mean infused contemplation—the classical mystical experience of the felt presence of God—as in the following: "Whenever I experienced contemplative prayer, there was absolutely no doubt that I was in God's presence. The silence was of varying degrees, sometimes so deep that the mind could not even think, other times a bit more shallow as in the prayer of quiet."[2] In other places, the words are used more fluidly and less restrictively, as in the title of William H. Shannon's article— "Contemplative Prayer, Contemplation" in the *New Dictionary of Catholic Spirituality*. This article equates the two and surveys their historical development in a variety of meanings. Thomas Keating follows this usage in reference to Centering Prayer, perhaps the most popular form of contemplative prayer in our country today, equating the two as a "resting in God" that is open to all seekers of good will.

As a step toward defining the two terms in their contemporary context, I propose a distinction between contemplative prayer and contemplation: Contemplative prayer is the way,

---

1. John Main, *Talks on Meditation* (Montreal, 1979), 10.
2. Philip St. Romain, in the newsletter *Christian Prayer and Contemplation Forum* 8 (April 1997): 4. Address: P.O. Box 520, Chiloquin, Oregon 97624.

contemplation the terminus. This is not common usage. Nor is the distinction an adequate one, for there is certainly an intimate and organic connection between the way and the goal: one includes the other. Contemplative prayer is designed to achieve contemplation; what begins as contemplative prayer becomes contemplation. But I make the distinction for clarity's sake, not just to be splitting hairs.

Contemplative prayer begins with one's own activity, however simple and non-discursive, and it seeks silence before God, silent presence beyond thinking, imagining, and making affections. Edwina Gately has seized the genius of contemplative prayer in the following psalm titled "Let your God love you."[3]

Be silent.	Let your God	He only wants to
Be still.	Look upon you.	Look upon you
Alone. Empty.	That is all.	With his love.
Before your God.	He knows.	Quiet.
Say nothing.	He understands.	Still.
Ask nothing.	He loves you with	Be.
Be silent.	An enormous love.	Let your God
Be still.		Love you.

This poetic catalogue intimates what happens when people practice Centering Prayer or Christian Meditation. Are these prayer forms contemplation? Yes; they seek and find the experience of God's love and presence, and this is contemplation in the general sense. Neither prayer form has directly in mind the experience of classical infused contemplation.

William Johnston shows great insight in seeing the typical forms of contemplative prayer today as neither Eastern nor Western, but something new in the world, "a third way, 'a tertium quid,' . . . the Gospel of Jesus Christ in a new world." He lists some of the methods and then relates them to mystical prayer in the strict sense:

---

3. Edwina Gateley, *There Was No Path So I Trod One: Poems* (Trabuco Canyon, Calif.: Source Books; 1996), 17. Reprinted with permission of the publisher.

For the fact is that everywhere we see Christians of all ages and cultures sitting quietly in meditation. Some sit before a crucifix or an ikon in one-pointed meditation. Others sit and breathe as they look at the tabernacle. Others practice mindfulness, awareness of God in their surroundings. Others recite the mantra to the rhythm of their own breath. Others influenced by Zen or yoga or vipassana open their minds and hearts to the presence of God in the universe. Others just talk to God. . . .

Assuredly these ways cannot immediately be called mystical. But they are gateways to mysticism. They all lead to silence and to the wordless state that St. Teresa calls the prayer of quiet to the higher mansions.[4]

William Johnston has thus related contemplative prayer to contemplation in a heuristic fashion and with a distinction. Today's methods of contemplative prayer are not automatically mystical, but they are steps in that direction. The word *contemplation* has no clear boundaries in common usage today.

Contemplation as a category is generally broader and less precise than infused contemplation in the strict sense. Contemplation in the *Spiritual Exercises* of St. Ignatius, for example, is more inclusive than Teresa's prayer of quiet or John of the Cross's infused knowledge and love. William McNamara's well-known description of contemplation as "a long, loving look at the real" fits the contemplative prayer forms Johnston refers to above (and fits infused contemplation as well). The phrase appealed to the Jesuit Walter Burghardt because of its down-to-earth, fully human, and existential quality. It became the title of his famous article on contemplation, which is a moving reflection, not on the contemplation of Teresa or John, but on the bodily, emotional, and spiritual awareness of concrete singulars in creation and their rootedness in God.[5] It is the mindfulness in William Johnston's list.

There are exceptions to this generic usage. In the Carmelite and the Dominican traditions, contemplation means infused

---

4. William Johnston, *Mystical Theology* (London: Harper Collins, 1995), 134.

5. Walter J.Burghardt, "Contemplation: A Long, Loving Look at the Real," in *Church,* no. 5 (Winter 1989): 14–17.

contemplation. Occasionally, of course, writers within these traditions use the term in a broader meaning. But in Teresa of Ávila and John of the Cross, contemplation is specific and exclusive. It is the general, loving, obscure experience of God that begins with the prayer of quiet or the passive dark night of the senses. It is infused knowledge and love; it is mystical; it is a pure gift of God that cannot be achieved by human effort under the ordinary working of grace. There are other forms of infused contemplation in the strict sense besides this apophatic experience, but all of them have in common the passive and mystical quality.

In today's spiritual theology, the distinction between active and passive prayer tends to be downplayed. Long ago, Thomas Merton rejected the distinction between infused and acquired contemplation as being irrelevant. The experience is the thing, not an abstract explanation of its principles. Moreover, the mystical or grace-character of the entire spiritual life is being emphasized in many sectors, for example, in twelve-step spirituality and in writings inspired by the theology of Karl Rahner.

For Karl Rahner, all experience of God is the expression of faith and love, all of it is rightly called mystical, and all knowledge and love of God are infused. Not only prayer experiences, but even the mundane experiences of average Christians which are products of faith are movements of the Holy Spirit and constitute "ordinary mysticism" or the "mysticism of everyday life." In Rahner's view, what has been designated as infused contemplation in the tradition is a high degree of the same one basic experience of loving faith. The classical mystical experience of the saints remains "extraordinary," not because of its principles, but because of its perfection and rarity. Theologically, the experience of God in meditation, in human activity, or in classical infused contemplation are all the same one gift of God working within us, the same one reality different not in kind but in degree.

This theology relativizes the inquiry of this paper. In light of Karl Rahner, it is less important whether we are dealing with a broad or narrow definition of contemplation. His theology allows us to use the term contemplation inclusively for both ordinary and extraordinary contemplation. Rahner's theology does not erase the considerable differences between the two on the experiential level, and this is terrain of our inquiry. We are asking questions that are important for spiritual direction, whatever the explanations offered by systematic theology.

Rahner does make the immense contribution of helping us to see the spiritual life as a unity and to think in terms of process, development, and transitions. Contemplative prayer and contemplation fit into the four steps of *lectio divina.* The first three steps—reading, meditation, and prayer—are obviously active, and the fourth step, contemplation, indicates rest, quiet, and receptivity. Where does the contemplative prayer we are discussing fit in this conspectus? I like to locate it between the third and fourth steps of the whole process. It is a specially designed form of active prayer, consisting in simplified efforts to quiet down, to be attentive, and to be open to the divine influence. But it is rightly called "contemplative" since it anticipates and moves as quickly as possible to its terminus of resting in the Lord. In this perspective, it is easy to see why most writers identify contemplative prayer and contemplation as the same thing. One of the classic definitions of the fourth step of *lectio divina* comes from the twelfth-century *Ladder of the Monks* by Guiges II, which describes contemplation as happening "when the mind is in some sort lifted up to God and held above itself, so that it tastes the joys of everlasting sweetness."[6] This flowery language can well be describing infused contemplation; but it is also obvious that as the terminus of the process of *lectio divina,* it is then the ordinary experience of prayer.[7]

Meditation and Contemplation

FURTHER LIGHT CAN be thrown on the nature of contemporary contemplative prayer if we look at the traditional Catholic teaching about meditation and contemplation. Does contemplative prayer

---

6. Cited in Lawrence S. Cunningham and Keith J. Egan, *Christian Spirituality* (New York: Paulist, 1996), 93–94.

7. *A Monk of New Clairvaux: Don't You Belong to Me?* (New York: Paulist Press, 1979), 114–49.

in the form of Centering Prayer or Christian Meditation belong to meditation or to contemplation as these words are used in the Catholic tradition? Meditation is active prayer, discursive in method, in the control of the practitioner and available to all persons of good will. Contemplation is knowledge by way of love, the fruit of a search, the experience of God's love poured forth in our hearts by the Holy Spirit who is given us (see Rom. 5:5). Contemplation is given, as pure gift, when the person is disposed to receive it. These descriptions leave intact what we have said about the two kinds of contemplation.

Jurgen Moltmann offers an analysis of meditation and contemplation that clarifies the distinction. Meditation, for Moltmann, is reflection on the Cross, the paschal mystery, the gospel message of Christ-for-us. Contemplation too is biblical and Christological, because it is the awareness of the knowledge and love evoked in one's self by this reflection, and hence it is a return to self-awareness. Contemplation is the awareness of Christ-in-us:

> I understand by meditation the loving, sympathetic and participatory recognition of something, and by contemplation the reflecting coming to awareness of oneself in this meditation. He [sic] who meditates sinks himself in the object of his meditation. He is absorbed in it and "forgets himself." The object of his meditation in turn sinks itself in him. Then in contemplation he comes again to self-awareness. He registers the changes in himself.[8]

Contemplation, then, is the experience of what God is doing in my own being in Christ. It is what is left over in my body, soul, and spirit as the aftermath of my meditation. There are moments of contemplation in every meditation. Such moments, prolonged and deliberately indulged to the exclusion of further meditation (that is, further thinking, imagining, or making affections), are what the contemporary methods mean by contemplation. They

---

8. "Theology of Mystical Experience," *Scottish Journal of Theology* 32 (1980): 505. Moltmann cites Thomas Merton, *Contemplation in a World of Action,* and *The Cloud of Unknowing* for these distinctions, and also J. V. Taylor, *The Go-Between God* (London, 1972), whose revealing thesis is that "the thought of the awareness of awareness [is] an experience of the Holy Spirit."

are the fourth act in *lectio divina* directly and immediately pursued as the total intent of the prayer.

In this frame of reference, we can see that Centering Prayer and Christian Meditation do not fit handily in the category of either meditation or contemplation. They are something new in contemplative prayer practice. Thomas Keating has emphasized that Centering Prayer is not *lectio divina,* but a form of prayer designed to give new life to *lectio* and to the whole Christian life. Centering Prayer is one's own doing, but it is contemplative in its very structure. It is ordered directly to the heart of the matter, contemplation itself. It depends on the prior endowment of grace, the Divine Indwelling, and the presence of faith, hope, and charity. One needs to have put on the Lord Jesus Christ through the word of God heard, appropriated, and welcomed through the agency of meditation in its many forms, through liturgy and common prayer, through spiritual disciplines and community. Centering Prayer or any legitimate form of contemplative prayer comes along to harvest the fruits, fine-tune the process of Christian living, highlight the gift aspect of the whole journey, and give one rest and enjoyment in this new life in Christ. Centering Prayer pulls the spiritual life together and goes far beyond the "morsels of spirituality," which John of the Cross calls the moments of contemplation that are the fruit of active meditation or the underlying grace in psychic phenomena like visions and locutions.

Teresa of Ávila and John of the Cross

HOW DOES THIS analysis relate to the teaching of Teresa of Ávila and John of the Cross? Teresa's "active recollection," which she developed out of her own life experience and described in doctrinal terms in *The Way of Perfection* (chaps. 28–29), is a transitional prayer form between meditation and contemplation and very similar to modern contemplative prayer.[9] Active

---

9. The present author has discussed Teresa's early personal prayer style in "St. Teresa of Ávila and Centering Prayer," *Carmelite Studies 3* (Washington, D.C.: Institute of Carmelite Studies, 1984), 191–211.

recollection is the equivalent of Centering Prayer, the image or memory from the gospel focusing the attention just as the sacred word does in Centering Prayer. For Teresa, contemplation begins in the Fourth Mansions, both of which are mystical. In the imagery of the waters, contemplation happens when the bucket or aqueduct is no longer necessary, and the water bubbles up from an inner spring. Active recollection is the personal cultivation and enjoyment of the Divine Presence through one's own efforts. It is the door to the mystical prayer of quiet and union as indeed are Centering Prayer and Christian Meditation in due time.

John of the Cross has no counterpart to Teresa's active recollection or to the new forms of contemplative prayer. The first fruits of contemplation are experienced in the passive dark night of the senses, when the person cannot pray in the old ways, finds no satisfaction in any particular goods, and has a profound yearning for God. Before that time, one is to use one's faculties in the practice of meditation. John has no transitional form between meditation and contemplation; the pray-er is praying one or the other. He does counsel simple attention and loving awareness at the onset of the dark night. While it is tempting to identify this practice with our contemplative prayer, the advice applies to a different situation. The simple attention presupposes the presence of God's special action infusing light and love in a subtle way, at times so subtle the Divine action may go unrecognized.[10] We are dealing with the beginning of infused contemplation in the strict sense. The three signs will validate its presence, and the person gives a loving attention that is passive, "without efforts . . . as a person who opens his eyes with loving attention."[11] For St.

---

10. According to Max Huot de Longchamp, the subtlety of the grace of infused contemplation is partially due to the fact that the infused light and love go directly to the object without any return to the self. Huot gives a convincing analysis of St. John of the Cross for this opinion. Infused contemplation in this view does not find its full explanation in the analysis of Moltmann above. See *Saint Jean de la Croix: Pour Lire le Docteur Mystique* (Paris: Fac-editions, 1991), 164.

11. St. John of the Cross, *Living Flame* 3.33.

John of the Cross, contemplation is pure gift and simply received: there is no room for active collaboration. John's contemplation is not the immediate horizon of contemporary, contemplative prayer forms.[12]

Concluding Observations

THROUGHOUT THIS PAPER, we have seen that contemplative prayer and contemplation have two levels or degrees of perfection, which we have designated as ordinary and extraordinary or general and infused. Their identity depends on how fully they emanate from the human heart, which is the seat of all valid prayer. The *Catechism of the Catholic Church* describes the role of the heart in these words:

> The heart is our hidden center, beyond the grasp of our reason and of others; only the Spirit of God can fathom the human heart and know it fully. The heart is the place of decision, deeper than our psychic drives. It is the place of truth, where we choose life or death. It is the place of encounter, because as image of God we live in relation; it is the place of covenant. (N.2563)

The level of the heart is the realm of the spirit (as opposed to the sensibility) in John of the Cross. It is the ground of our being, the fine point of the soul, the center that holds our whole being, the place where God dwells within us. It is not a physical place, but a level of our operation in which God is the agent and we are receivers. God comes in fullness when we are empty in our hearts. God comes in proportion to our openness, our freedom, our poverty of spirit. God as Holy Spirit possesses us and

---

12. The dark night is the entree to the infused contemplation of John of the Cross. But even the dark night has a wide sense that does not include the presence of contemplation as described in the third sign of *The Ascent of Mount Carmel 2.13.4*, according to a tape titled "Are There Contemplatives Today?" and published by his own Inner Growth Ministries in Chiloquin, Oregon. Without that express contemplation, the person needs to make acts of faith and love and not be simply idle in the prayer. This is to avoid the error of quietism. There is no contradiction here to the conclusions of this paper.

forms us in the image of the Son. This is the work of grace within us. The Spirit is operative in all good actions and completely takes over when we are acting on the level of the spirit, when we let go of ourselves in some complete fashion. This action of God within us is contemplation, and it takes place in proportion to our poverty of spirit. This poverty of spirit is practically the same thing as the contemplation itself.

Centering Prayer and Christian Meditation are more fully prayer from the heart than is discursive prayer. They attempt to move the spiritual life to deeper levels than exterior, psychic, or conceptual activity. They take their practitioners to the center, to true authentic and mature spirituality beyond mere sensibility. But, unlike infused contemplation in the strict sense, they are not mystical or fully passive forms; they have an active element and they depend on human collaboration.

The dynamics of Centering Prayer and Christian Meditation are similar, but they differ in emphasis. Both call the person to enter within, to move to the realm of silence and solitude, the level of the heart, to let go of thinking and imagining or controlling, and to cultivate simple presence to the Divine Presence. One is lovingly attentive to the Divine Indwelling.

Centering Prayer suggests the saying of the sacred word, some simple word like *Jesus,* as a way to express consent to God's working in the soul. It is the response to God's love, accepting and welcoming the action of God. The sacred word as a symbol of the pray-er's intention to consent to God's presence and action within us is to be used when one finds oneself off into other thoughts, feelings, memories, or perceptions.

In Christian Meditation, on the other hand, the mantra, which is usually the word MA-RA-NA-THA ("Come, Lord Jesus"), is spoken throughout the prayer as an effort, not only to be totally attentive, but to be empty and silent and alone before God. The mantra is the instrument that creates the emptiness; it hollows out the soul. Meditation takes seriously the teaching of the masters that creating silence and emptiness is the best invitation to the Spirit. In the dyad of poverty and contemplation, Christian Meditation goes through the door of poverty. Centering Prayer takes the other door of simple, loving presence to God. In the end, the two methods are searching for the same fullness and emptiness.

My sense is that other popular forms of contemplative prayer follow the same lines that we have drawn for the two exemplars. These prayer-forms are gifts for our time, making more available the entrance to a deeper life with God. A figure from twelve-step experience may help us understand the widespread attraction of these new forms of contemplative prayer and, at the same time, serve as a bridge to St. John of the Cross. The figure is this: It used to be said that a person had to "hit bottom" before he or she were a candidate for the twelve-step program. Today, I am told, clients are advised to "raise the bottom" and begin the program before a crisis occurs. Something like this may be working in contemplative prayer today. The forms do not presuppose infused contemplation or even an advanced spiritual state, and they teach the person to be appropriately active in the prayer. And they promise a fuller outpouring ot the Spirit. In this time of ours, contemporary contemplative prayer forms are a providential gift of the Holy Spirit.

4 ❀

Centering Prayer as Radical Consent

CYNTHIA BOURGEAULT

Thomas Keating, a principal shaper and a chief teacher of the Centering Prayer movement, emphasizes that this form of Christian meditational prayer is not an innovation, but rather "a further attempt to present the teaching of earlier times in an updated format."[1] Certainly, there is truth in his assertion. Keating views Centering Prayer not as a meditational technique but as a modern approach to contemplative prayer, an activity viewed in the Benedictine tradition as the final stage of *lectio divina* (the "divine reading") of scripture. Keating has placed Centering Prayer firmly within the ancient tradition of Christian monastic practice. His emphasis on the Christian roots of Centering Prayer help forestall the criticism that Centering Prayer is nothing more than the introduction of Eastern meditational practices into Western Christianity.

---

1. Thomas Keating, *Intimacy with God* (New York: Crossroad, 1994), 45. These "earlier times" being based primarily upon the fourteenth-century *The Cloud of Unknowing* and the writings of St. John of the Cross.

While there may be sound reasons for emphasizing the traditional aspects of Centering Prayer, I want to underscore its significant innovations. Centering Prayer may call to mind the traditional wedding advice: "Something old, something new, something borrowed, something blue." This article will focus on the "something new." The externals may look similar to other forms of meditational prayer, but Keating has discovered, deep in the internals, a crucial shift of emphasis that distinguishes it from its contemporary counterparts, such as Christian Meditation as developed and promulgated by John Main,[2] the traditional approaches to contemplative prayer advocated in the monastic practice of *lectio divina* and in the Orthodox tradition expounded in the *Philokalia*.[3]

Stated in its most emphatic form, my argument is that Keating may have discovered Christianity's own alchemist's stone: the catalytic spiritual substances proper to the Christian spiritual path. When consistently and coherently practiced, Centering Prayer makes it possible to do the gospel—not metaphorically but as a powerful path of transformation. Evidence of this role becomes increasingly clear as the Centering Prayer movement, now twenty years old, develops an increasingly sophisticated self-awareness and a growing number of practitioners whose lives bear witness to the transformational power of Centering Prayer.

Is Centering Prayer Meditation?

MEDITATION IS GENERALLY known as deep, continuous reflection. It is practiced in many religions with a variety of aims, often in

2. John Main, *Christian Meditation* (Montreal: Benedictine Priory of Montreal, 1952). Main has numerous other books, tapes, and videos on the subject as well.

3. The *Philokalia*, a collection of writings from the early fathers, is a major sourcebook of Orthodox spirituality, particularly the traditions associated with Mt. Athos. Compiled in the eighteenth century, it has yet to be fully translated from Greek into English. The most accessible English "sampler" is E. Kadloubovsky and C. F. H. Palmer, trans., *Writings from the Philokalia on Prayer of the Heart* (London and Boston: Faber and Faber, 1951, 1992).

conjunction with techniques for breathing, posture, or the ordering of one's thoughts. A faculty member at the Shalem Institute for Spiritual Direction is reported to have asked if Centering Prayer is meditation, and it is a very good question. The answer, as far as I can see, is neither yes or no exactly, but Centering Prayer's innovation resides in the "maybe no" consideration.

Maybe yes. Centering Prayer belongs unquestionably to the larger category of meditation because it requires an initial willingness to break identification with the surface tension of the mind. This is like jumping off a diving board; it entails the risk that something else exists below the jumble of thoughts, emotions, and memories that float down our stream of consciousness. That is, there is something deeper, more permanent, and more present that will only be found by a dissociation from the tyranny of the surface. All meditation begins with this fundamental act of trust.

Maybe no. Once this initial plunge off the diving board has been ventured, how does one navigate the depths? How does one keep from being drawn back up to the surface by the attraction of thoughts or the terror of the depths. In answering these questions, Centering Prayer's contributions augment and even move somewhat counter to conventional meditational wisdom.

Most meditational methods offered by both Eastern and Western traditions work with the property of attention. One is asked to put one's focus on something: the breath, a mantra, or a bodily sensation (for example, "I place attention on my right arm, my breathing, and so on). When a thought beckons from the surface of the mind, attention holds one firmly in the present. In fact, with a sufficiently focussed will, attention functions as a kind of thought-suppressant, forcing down the turbulent upwelling of associations from the deeper levels of the psyche. By concentrating the mind on a single object or task, one breaks through the dissipative quality of the untrained mind (a "monkey mind," the Buddhists call it), and one begins to build a vessel that can collect and retain the higher, deeper energy of self (or God) that is normally squandered on the gristmill of the personal "I."

Centering Prayer works with an entirely different property—not attention but *intention*.[4] While the practice makes use of a "sacred word" as a touchstone for meditation, its use is fundamentally different from a "concentrative" (i.e., attention-based) method. The word is not repeated constantly as a focal point for attention. It has neither an emotional content (as in the "Jesus Prayer" of Eastern Orthodox tradition) nor a physiological basis (as in the classic mantra, which is in essence a vibration intended to induce physiological changes within the body). Rather, it simply serves as the reminder of one's intent for the duration of the prayer period to relinquish attachment to one's surface flow of thoughts and associations and to rest instead in the undifferentiated presence of God.

Workshops introducing Centering Prayer hammer this point home: it is the essence of the method. People who come assuming that a "good" meditation is one in which the mind is quiet quickly learn otherwise. The power of Centering Prayer is contained not in suppressing thoughts ("making the mind a blank") but in the will. One might also call it, for reasons that will shortly become clear, the willingness to let go of thoughts as they arise and return to the sacred word as a symbol of one's consent to rest in God. Keating has a story about a nun who complained to him at the end of the prayer period that her meditation had been a complete failure. "In twenty minutes," she said, "I must have had twenty thousand thoughts." Keating replied, "How wonderful. Twenty thousand opportunities to return to God." As beginning practitioners memorize the "four R's" of Centering Prayer—"Resist no thought, retain no thought, react to no thought, and return ever-so-gently to the sacred word"[5]—they gradually come to learn a method whose essence lies not in a strengthening of attention but in

---

4. Keating, *Intimacy with God*, 57. The chapter from which this was taken (55–65) tends to be the core teaching in all introductory workshops and lectures on Centering Prayer.

5. To my knowledge, although it regularly forms part of the teaching at Centering Prayer workshops, this formulation is unpublished. An earlier version, however, can be found in Keating, *Intimacy with God,* 64.

repeated, small reaffirmations of consent. On this small difference, a whole world turns.

Will and Willingness, Attention and Awareness

KEATING HIMSELF TENDS to be casual in the terms he uses for this key point. He uses "intention," "will," and "consent" more or less synonymously to point to the same basic element of receptivity. "Centering Prayer does not work with attention but with the faculty of will," he has remarked on many occasions. Following a line of thinking advanced by Gerald May, however, I want to insert a further distinction: Centering Prayer does not work with *will* but with *willingness*. Gerald May's *Will and Spirit* has become an indispensable handbook for those following a Christian contemplative path.[6] While having little to say about Centering Prayer explicitly (since it was still in its infancy in 1982), the book lays the best groundwork I know for understanding the larger significance of this prayer form.

Shying away from "will" as too monolithic a term, May (who is both a psychiatrist and a spiritual director) proposes that will is always encountered in one of two modes, willfulness or willingness.

> Willingness and willfulness cannot be explained in a few words, for they are very subtle qualities, often overlapping and very often confused with each other. But we can begin by saying that willingness implies a surrendering of one's self-separateness, an entering-into, an immersion in the deepest processes of life itself. It is a realization that one already is a part of some ultimate cosmic process and it is a commitment to participate in that process. In contrast, willfulness is the setting of oneself apart from the fundamental essence of life in an attempt to master, direct, control, or otherwise manipulate existence. More simply, willing-ness is saying yes to the mystery of being alive in each moment. Willfulness is saying no, or perhaps more commonly, "Yes, but . . ."[7]

---

6. Gerald G. May, *Will and Spirit: A Contemplative Psychology* (San Francisco: HarperSanFrancisco, 1982).

7. Ibid., 5–6.

In making this distinction, May points out the essential difference in feeling—composition and direction—of these two aspects of will. Willingness is essentially openness; it collects around it such terms as surrender, vulnerability, self-abandonment, and adoration. The direction of willingness is *pull:* being drawn higher or deeper. *Willfulness* is closed; it collects around it such terms as effort, manipulation, control, and competence. The direction of willfulness is *push:* an impetus outward from a firm center. One might say, then, that willingness tends in the direction of "No-Self," a laying-down of individual boundaries before a larger connectedness. Willfulness tends in the direction of "Super-Self," the extension of one's individual boundaries to include more and more of the universe.

Similarly, May distinguishes between awareness and attention, defining the latter as a subset of the former. "Awareness," he claims, "is that part of consciousness that is noticed, recognized, sensed, or in some way affected by a person" in which "no specific sensation takes priority [but] all are received with equal openness." He gives as an example the generalized appreciation for the beauty of a starry winter night. By contrast, "attention is awareness that is restricted and alert," requiring "a limitation or restriction of the range of awareness, a shutting-out of so-called distractions." Attention is, in short, a reduction in the degree of openness of awareness.[8]

What causes this reduction, this tightening of focus? Clearly, it is willfulness. Intent on one purpose, we limit our range of perceptivity to that purpose. If we step out into that starry night to fetch the evening paper, as May points out, we are unlikely to notice the beauty surrounding us.

From the following, we can take one further step in our list of associations:

Willingness as surrender, vulnerability, self-abandonment, and adoration: *awareness* (a "pull").

Willfulness as effort, manipulation, control, and competence: *attention* (a "push").

---

8. Ibid., 47.

Such a schematic allows us to see clearly the different paths available to us. Centering Prayer works with the property of willingness; traditional "concentrative" methods of meditation work with attention, that is, with willfulness. I do not mean to oversimplify the process. All meditational discipline comes around eventually to what May would call awareness: an open, undifferentiated perception of the dynamic ground.[9] In the initial territory to be traversed, however, before awareness is established in its own orbit, the words describing "willing-ness" seem to strike a more fundamental resonance with the heart of Christianity as set forth in the gospels and as celebrated in the liturgy. In fact, there is a much richer correspondence between the inner path and the outer path.

When I first came upon May's definitions, I viewed them with suspicion. I was well aware of the venerable place that attention holds in virtually every spiritual tradition of the world. Nowhere is attention more important than in the *Philokalia*, the most comprehensive exposition of the "inner way" available to serious Christian seekers. I viewed May's negative appraisal of attention as idiosyncratic. I have since changed my mind, in a large part because of continued work with Centering Prayer. As I now see it, attention has acquired its respected place in religious tradition primarily because it has been accepted as axiomatic that this is the only available starting point. It seems to be the only means at hand to break the surface tension of the mind, the necessary precondition for the emergence of the heart. The Eastern Orthodox tradition makes this manifestly clear in the teachings of *The Art of Prayer*. Because "the mind is inseparable from attention," we are urged to stand before God with "the mind in the heart."[10]

> The essential thing is for the mind to unite with the heart at prayer [with] an unhurried repetition of the prayer, a brief pause after each prayer, quiet and steady breathing, and enclosing the mind in

---

9. Eastern and Western writers variously refer to "dynamic ground." See Ibid., 172, regarding "root spiritual energy."

10. Timothy Ware, ed., *The Art of Prayer: An Orthodox Anthology*, E. Kadloubovsky and E. M. Palmer, trans. (London: Faber, 1951, 1992), 189.

the words of the prayer. With the aid of such means we can easily achieve a certain degree of attention. Before long the heart begins to be in sympathy with the attention of the mind as it prays. Little by little the sympathy of the heart with the mind begins to change into a union of mind and heart. The essential, indispensable element in prayer is attention. Without attention there is no prayer.[11]

Centering Prayer, however, suggests otherwise. In point of fact, underlying all attention there must be the element of intention. What would support the effort to "pay attention" if there were not already an underlying yearning of the will? This is an insight beautifully expressed in *The Cloud of Unknowing* as a "naked intent direct to God."[12] Centering Prayer bypasses the spiritual substance of attention. As the Philokalia asserts, such attention is inseparable from the mind, the seat of our sense of alienation, fear, and pushiness.[13] This makes it possible to work directly—and from the outset—with the substance of consent, which may well be the heart's native language.

It is this insight, I believe, that is at the center of Thomas Keating's remarkable contribution to the recovery of the Christian contemplative path. Essentially, he has shattered a sacred cow of meditational pedagogy: that one must begin from the access point of attention. To the contrary, he argues, consent is an equally legitimate and perhaps more effective starting point. The weight of evidence seems to be on his side. Time and time again, I have watched Christian seekers who have failed repeatedly to develop any consistency in an attention-based practice take to Centering Prayer like a duck to water. Early on in the practice—sometimes even on their first attempt—beginners who grasp the principle of consent and embrace it with a real inner willingness can and do experience deep periods of contemplative rest.

---

11. Ibid., 104.

12. Ira Progoff, ed., *The Cloud of Unknowing* (New York: Dell; London: Rider, 1957), 76.

13. Ware, *The Art of Prayer,* 65, 83.

The Path

A FULLY ARTICULATED spiritual path always incorporates both inner and outer aspects. The inner path is the spiritual practice that works at the deepest recesses of the heart. In addition, there is an outer path that extends this work into the world as a channel for both growth and manifestation. Without such a connecting link, meditation becomes, in Keating's words, merely "a high class tranquilizer."[14] For a practice based on attention, the path is mindfulness. For a practice based on consent, the path is surrender.

Whatever the practical advantages of a meditational prayer based on consent, the real payoff is its powerful congruence with a basic attitude of Christianity in the direction of ever-deepening surrender: "Not my will be done, Lord, but thine" (Luke 22:42). One of the difficulties of re-establishing a meditational praxis at the core of Christian spirituality is that the generally stated goals of such a practice (to reduce stress, to develop inner attention, to access higher states of consciousness) receive little scriptural validation. Too often, practitioners look upon meditation as a "place" where they go to find God, a kind of reservoir of quiet at which they "tank up" during their sittings and from which they draw during the hurly-burly of the day. This attitude toward meditation heightens the contrast between their most intimate experience of God and the demands of life in the world.

It is not so with Centering Prayer. To be sure, practitioners of the prayer do generally experience deep periods of interior quiet, but Keating makes it clear that God is not found in the quiet per se but in the action of consent itself, a consent to whatever emerges. As such, the prayer period becomes an intensive inner laboratory, as it were, for the practice of consent. If an emotionally charged thought, a pleasant memory, or a painful upheaval from the unconscious appears on the surface of consciousness and momentarily attracts attention, the instructions are always the same: "Resist no thought, retain no thought, react to no thought, and return ever-so-gently to the sacred word." In

---

14. Keating, *Intimacy with God*, 105.

this inner laboratory, practitioners begin to make the discovery that they are not their thoughts and emotions, that feelings no matter how strong and frightening may be weathered simply by the consent to drop them and rest in the bare presence of God.

This powerful discovery forms the basis for work in daily life. If one can drop a negative or charged thought during the inner laboratory of prayer, is it not possible to do the same in daily life? The experience of consent during a period of prayer enables one to let go of attachment to one's thoughts, feelings, and impressions. These are things that normally feed the grist-mill of self. That same consent becomes the basis in the outer world for practical work on oneself. With repeated practice, one can learn to identify and let go of one's "emotional programs for happiness" (as Keating calls them) when they arise as anger, fear, righteous indignation, despair, or some other form. The "Open Mind, Open Heart" practice, taught at special Centering Prayer workshops, offers intensive training in this form of self-surrender. It is a three-step method of focussing on the particular afflictive emotion arising, *welcoming it* (to avoid the trap of repression so fatal to religious consciousness), and letting it go (insofar as that is possible). There is a connection made between letting go of thoughts as the touchstone of meditation, letting go of immature and selfish emotional programs as the touchstone for practical work on self, and letting go of self as the touchstone of the gospel path. In all of this, a clear pattern of sympathetic vibration is established, a "letting go" at each level that reinforces all levels.

As this happens, prayer and "the world" are no longer opposed but grow closer together. In the process, one gradually learns that one can "pray without ceasing" in spite of the demands of modern life. This occurs by "consenting without ceasing" to the presence and action of God in each moment regardless of the circumstances of life. Thus, far from leading away from a scriptural Christianity, Centering Prayer points toward the heart of it by illuminating from within its core motion: self-surrender in loving trust. Meditational prayer is not grafted onto Christianity but arises out of its very matrix, and the

Christian paradigm for spiritual transformation becomes consistent across the board:

meditational mode: consent, willingness
psychological mode: letting go
gospel emphasis: surrender, self-giving
worship mode: adoration
prayer mode: trust
destination: true self

Toward Attention of the Heart

NEARLY A MILLENNIUM ago, the Orthodox spiritual master Saint Simeon the New Theologian wrote an important treatise on "Three Methods of Attention and Prayer."[15] His observations may have considerable bearing on locating Centering Prayer within the wider context of Christian interior prayer and pointing toward its capacities for sustaining inner transformation.

The first method of attention in prayer, as Simeon described it, is essentially arousal of affective prayer through visualization and discursive meditation:

> If a man stands at prayer and, raising his hands, his eyes and his mind to heaven, keeps in mind Divine thoughts, imagines celestial blessings, hierarchies of angels and dwellings of the saints, assembles briefly in his mind all that he has learnt from the Holy Scriptures and ponders over all this while at prayer, gazing up to heaven, and thus inciting his soul to longing and love of God, at times even shedding tears and weeping, this will be the first method of attention and prayer.[16]

This is essentially the charismatic prayer of our Western tradition or, in *lectio divina,* the delicate movement from *meditatio* to *oratio.* The problem, Simeon asserts, is that it relies on a high level of excitement of the external faculties, which is ultimately self-delusional and can become addictive, leading one to depend on lights, sweet scents, voices, and "other like phenomena" as

---

15. Kadloubovsky and Palmer, *Writings from the Philokalia,* 152–61.
16. Ibid., 153.

evidence of the presence of God. "If then such a man gives him-self up to utter silence," Simeon adds bluntly, "he can scarcely avoid going out of his mind."[17]

The second method is self-examination and the collecting of thoughts "so that they cease to wander"—the classic methodology of a practice based on attention. "With great labor and self-exertion [he] strives to come back into himself," Simeon observes. This process involves evoking dimensions of effort, control, manipulation, and willfulness, all of which we men-tioned earlier as the occupational hazards of an attention-based practice. The fatal flaw in this method, Simeon observes, is that such a practitioner "remains in the head, whereas evil thoughts are generated in the heart." If he further compounds his problem by vainglory—the conviction that he can control attention—"the unhappy man works in vain and will lose his reward for ever."[18]

Simeon designated the third method as *attention of the heart.* He described this method in the following terms:

> You should observe three things before all else: freedom from all cares, not only cares about bad and vain but even about good things . . . ; *your* conscience should be clear in all things so that it denounces you in nothing; and you should have complete *absence of passionate attachment,* so that your thought inclines towards nothing worldly.[19]

Simeon's words above describe Centering Prayer. As one attempts to "resist no thought, retain no thought, react to no thought," one is actually gaining experience in small (but utterly real) increments toward "freedom from all cares" and the "absence of passionate attachment." This is Simeon's "attention of the heart," which he states is inseparable from true prayer and true conversion. What Thomas Keating has really succeeded in doing is to give meditational form to Simeon's "attention of the heart." He has thereby provided a powerful new access point to the traditional wisdom of the Christian inner path.

---

17. Ibid., 153.
18. Ibid., 154.
19. Ibid., 158.

5 ❋

"Oh, Freedom!": Exploring the Mystic and the Prophet in African-American Spirituality

EUGENE TAYLOR SUTTON

I was reared in black Baptist congregations in rural North Carolina and in Washington, D.C., which is to say that I sang, cried, clapped, and shouted my way into faith. Bold, bluesy, and vibrant, African-American culture values self-expression in its religion as well as in its art, music and, well, everyday conversation. One is not encouraged to sit still, quiet, and motionless in the company of others, and if this is done while the community is "having church," then prayers and exhortations are offered for the Spirit to visit that place more powerfully. Exuberant bursts of noise and speech often signify the presence of God in black church spirituality, much as they did in the story of the beginnings of the Christian movement at Pentecost as told in the second chapter of the Book of Acts.

How is it, then, that someone nurtured as a child on the milk of revivalist spirituality finds himself nourished by contemplative worship and Centering Prayer in his adult years? What is there in the African-American spiritual tradition that lays the groundwork for an authentic contemplative spirituality which incorporates the wisdom of the black fathers and mothers of the faith? This essay will explore these issues by analyzing the mystic and prophetic strands in the black religious religious experience and suggest how they converge into a spirituality that has sustained African Americans through slavery and oppression into liberation.

Definitions

SCHOLARS OF RELIGION frequently will describe religious experience as corresponding to two broad ways of knowing God, the "prophetic" and the "mystic." In the prophetic form of religious experience, the divine is encountered as a wholly "other" transcendent reality that is clearly distinct from the human personality. In the mystic form of experience of religion, the divine is discovered within the depths of the individual's consciousness. In the former, God is encountered outside of oneself; in the latter, God is encountered within oneself.

These typologies, of course, are abstractions; they are theological constructs which may be more usefully thought of as descriptive of religious tendencies rather than as precise definitions of one's religious experience. Broadly speaking, the prophetic type is characteristic of the monotheistic religions which originated from the area now called the Middle East, i.e., Judaism, Islam, and Christianity, and the mystic type characterizes the religious tradition of East and South Asia. In fact, however, these tendencies may be found to exist in some measure in a variety of traditions, and they cannot be viewed merely as polarities which clearly distinguish western from eastern religions.

Moreover, the two types both have a "this worldly" and an "other worldly" dimension to them. For instance, in sociologist Max Weber's classic typology, the result of any genuinely transcendent experience is that one separates oneself from the material world, existing in a realm in which time and space have no meaning. That experience can either send the person back into the world with a new insight and sense of mission, or it can result in the person wanting to stay in the "other world" while rejecting this one.[1]

Thus one can properly speak of an "other wordly propheticism" which seeks God "out there" to be sure—but "there" is in heaven and not on earth, giving rise to the criticism leveled at Christians of this type that they are so heavenly minded that they are no earthly good. Such a spirituality elevates the importance of the self but rejects the world, as God is perceived to have given up on the world apart from the salvation of individual souls. Similarly, there is an "other worldly mysticism" which retreats from the world, but also from undue attention being given to the individual self in the cosmic order. It is typified by the desire to limit any real engagement with the world to an absolute minimum in order to give oneself over totally to the inner search for Divine union.

"This worldly propheticism" is exemplified by the response of the prophet Isaiah to his transcendent vision in Isaiah 6:1–8. After encountering the Holy and being purged from his sin, Isaiah hears the voice of the Lord saying, "Whom shall I send, and who will go for us?" Isaiah responds, "Here I am! Send me." The prophet's spirituality clearly leads him to find the divine presence outside of himself, (i.e., God sits on a throne surrounded by holy attendants), and sends him out to do work in God's world.

The "this worldly mystic" gives himself or herself over to the inner search for God, but not at the expense of significant involvement in world concerns. The posthumous publication of the writings of Dag Hammarskjold, the former Secretary-General of the United Nations, sheds light on the inner spiritual journey of a man committed to working for peace among the nations. Thomas Merton, the Trappist monk, and Howard Thurman, the black clergyman and educator, are also known as Christian mystics who did not retreat from societal problems. It should not be

---

1. Max Weber, *The Sociology of Religion* (Boston: Beacon Press, 1963), 166–75.

overlooked that both Merton and Thurman were heavily influenced by the mystic traditions of Eastern religions—Buddhism for Merton, Hinduism for Thurman.

In light of these distinctions along the this worldly/other worldly axis, the prophetic and mystic typologies can best be understood as tools for examining the religious impulses which underlie the concern for societal relations and structures on the one hand and the concern for individual growth on the other. There is a continuum along a theoretical line from the personal to the social, from private piety to justice, from "micro" to "macro" discernment of God's presence and activity in, with, and among human beings. The popular notion of the Outward and Inward Journey is helpful here; *journey* emphasizes the activity involved in reaching a desired destination. If the common destination is God, then how do we reach God? The prophetic strand in African-American spirituality corresponds to the Outward Journey, and it answers that one must find God "out there" as God is found working in society. The mystic strand points to the Inward Journey: one finds God as God is found working within the individual personality.

Thus, the Prophet and the Mystic typify the social and the personal dimensions of religion. The prophets of the Old Testament spoke *for* God *to* the people—an inherently social act. The biblical prophetic messages spoke of the need for societal repentance in light of God's anger with injustice in the land. Similarly, the African-American community has not hesitated to consign the status of prophet to a host of black orators who were called to proclaim to the nation the intention of God to see an end to slavery, racial segregation, and all other forms of oppression.

The mystic tradition in black religion, although always present, is perhaps the least understood aspect of African-American piety, for reasons which I shall mention later. Nonetheless, an adequate description of it can be found in Webster's New Collegiate Dictionary's definition of mysticism: "the belief that direct knowledge of God can be attained through subjective experience (as intuition or insight); the experience of direct communion with ultimate reality." This kind of mysticism in African-American spirituality finds its highest expression in the life and writings of Howard Thurman.

What follows is a brief discussion of the development of the prophetic and mystic traditions in African-American Christianity in order to reveal how these strands weave together into a whole. Although mysticism and propheticism are clearly identifiable in the spirituality of black folk, they are not characteristically separable. Moreover, while divine transcendence in African American spirituality may be experienced in profoundly mystical ways and described in other-worldly terms, it does so in a way that does not deny the this-worldly intention of God for human beings to become deeply involved in the work of redeeming social structures.

The Prophetic Strand

THE PROPHETIC HERITAGE in black religion is a long and rich one, but much of its history has been undocumented until the late 1960s and early 1970s. The first scholar to examine the black religious experience as distinctly alien to "white Christianity" was Joseph Washington, who wrote *Black Religion* in 1964. It portrayed black propheticism at its best:

> Born in slavery, weaned in segregation and reared in discrimination, the religion of the Negro folk was chosen to bear the roles of both protest and relief. Thus, the uniqueness of black religion is the racial bond which seeks to risk its life for the elusive but ultimate goal of freedom and equality by means of protest and action. It does so through the only avenues to which its members have always been permitted a measure of access, religious convocations in the fields or in houses of worship.[2]

The most important contributor to the recovery of the prophetic tradition in black religious history is James Cone, who published his watershed *Black Theology and Black Power* in 1969. Dr. Cone, a professor of theology at Union Seminary in New York

---

2. Joseph R. Washington, *Black Religion* (Boston: Beacon Press, 1964), 33.

City, shocked the academic world by stating forcefully that the "white theology" taught in seminaries could not answer the questions that blacks were asking about God. The theology of the day was "created for comfortable white suburbia," and it had little to do with blacks in their struggle for dignity and freedom from racial oppression. What he called for was a Black Theology which would embrace black people's insistence that God was on their side in the struggle for Black Power.

Cone identified the black movement of liberation from racial, social, and economic oppression as the essence of the Christian gospel: "Black Power is the message of Christ Himself," and ". . . Black rebellion is a manifestation of God himself actively involved in the present day affairs of men for the purpose of liberating a people."[3] He developed further the relationship between theology and the social context in his later books, *A Black Theology of Liberation* (1970) and *God of the Oppressed* (1975). Other black theologians responded to Cone's bold initiative in theologizing about the black religious experience, scholars such as J. Deotis Roberts, Major Jones, Cornel West, and Gayraud Wilmore.

The heroes of the faith for the new black theologians were the nineteenth-century African-American Christians who led slave revolts and and underground movements for the abolition of slavery, represented by Nat Turner, Denmark Vesey, Harriet Tubman, and Sojourner Truth. They also turned to clergymen such as Henry Highland Garnet and David Walker, two of the most powerful black abolitionist orators, who urged black rebellion against slavery and compared the condition of Africans in this country with the Hebrew slaves in ancient Egypt. Another black minister, Henry McNeil Turner, foreshadowed Cone as a black theologian of liberation, boldly stating as early as the late 1890s that God was a Negro. The prophetic movement in black Christianity picked up steam in the mid-twentieth century with the Civil Rights Movement whose most prominent leader was Martin Luther King, Jr., although he was thought by many of the

---

3. James H. Cone, *Black Theology and Black Power* (New York: Seabury, 1969), 37–38.

black theologians to have not been radical enough in criticizing the spirituality of white Christianity that could allow persons to become comfortable with and seek God's blessing for personal and institutional racism.

Black Theology has been critiqued for its intemperate tone and for overlooking or not understanding the mystical dimensions of African-American spirituality. Cone's brother, Cecil Cone (also a theologian), has argued that without such an understanding Black Theology falls into the error of a "tendency to reduce black religion to a political ideology and . . . [failing] to see those elements in it that transcend political activity."[4] Thus Cecil Cone, while supportive of Black Theology, calls for it to return to its roots in the black church—not the academic institutions—which would allow its understandings to be shaped by the common spirituality of African-American worshipers.

Martin Marty, one of America's foremost church historians, has sounded a similar note, writing against "biased accounts of all black religion as liberating radical ideology . . .":

> Some recent scholars have tried to make it seem as if blacks used their religion almost entirely as a coding system to keep their own covert and subvert meaning systems alive. Not at all . . . they did have supernatural, otherworldly, and not always militant and liberating references. Very few peoples have used their spiritual sustenance only in order to organize for eventual revolution.[5]

The Mystic Strand

"Everything begins in mysticism and ends in politics," once uttered Charles Peguy, an early twentieth-century French Catholic spiritual and political leader. His statement is particularly true for the religion of the black church. African Americans have come to know that all so-called purely spiritual understandings have consequences for politics and social structures.

---

4. Cecil W. Cone, *The Identity Crisis in Black Theology* (Nashville, Tenn.: AMEC Press, 1975), 21.

5. Martin Marty, in the forward of Milton Sernett's *Black Religion and American Evangelicalism* (Metuchen, N.J.: Scarecrow Press, 1975), xv.

The mystical elements of African spirituality carried over into religious experience of the slaves when introduced to Christianity. Cecil Cone writes of "the drive that is everywhere manisfested in African societies that makes the supernatural a major focus of interest," a religious sense so ingrained in the African personality that the slave who was brought to America possessed already the spiritual resources needed to make meaning of his or her plight. Thus he asserts that "it may be said that Africans were not converted to Christianity but that they converted Christianity to themselves."[6]

Similarly, Gayraud Wilmore has contended that for some slaves, "the Spirit within" was superior even to the Bible as a guide to religious knowledge. This can be seen in the early rejection by African Americans of white preachers' use of the Scriptures to condone slavery and slave passivity. Illiterate and unschooled slaves *knew* that such teaching was foreign to the Christian gospel, not because of what some preacher might say from any book, but because such teaching was contrary to what God revealed to them in their hearts. As John Mbitit, a theologian from Africa, writes in African spirituality "there are no creeds to be recited; instead, the creeds are written in the heart of the individual, and each one is himself a living creed of his own religion."[7]

White Christians were often perplexed by this African mysticism which carried over into the the Christianity of the slaves. They considered it to be unbiblical, antinomian, and unorthodox—a not untrue judgment if the Euro–American faith of the missionaries was thought to be the norm for all Christians everywhere. Charles Colcock Jones, an early nineteenth-century white Presbyterian missionary, wrote the following upon observing the religious practices of newly converted slaves:

> True religion they are inclined to place in profession, in forms and ordinances, and in excited states of feeling. And true conversion, in dreams, visions, trances, voices—all bearing a perfect or striking

---

6. C. Cone, *The Identity Crisis in Black Theology,* 31.

7. John Mbiti, *African Religions and Philosophy* (New York: Anchor Press, 1970), 4.

resemblance to some form or type which has been handed down for generations. . . .[8]

The conversion experiences of slaves and freed blacks in the nineteenth century tell us much about the role of mysticism in African-American spirituality. In *Liberation and Human Wholeness*, Edward and Anne Wimberly carefully document the process by which blacks have made sense of the world by "turning around to God." Using oral and written accounts of actual conversion experiences, they have identified seven characteristics of the typical African-American religious conversion:

1) The inner experience of a mystical vision
2) The message of the vision expressed in a drama
3) The experiencer of the mystical experience is both observer and actor in the drama
4) Similar characters, images and themes appear in many of the experiences which have a transforming significance and meaning for the convert's life
5) The source of the experience is identified as Christian and supernatural
6) The convert finds his or her place in the world, helped by the new world view gained
7) There ensues a radical turnaround in thinking and behavior which is nurtured and acted out in Christian community.[9]

The description clearly distinguishes such conversions from those described in the white evangelical revivalist tradition. The black conversions were highly mystical in their beginnings, and yet they landed the convert firmly back into engagement with the world in which he or she was placed. That world was in desperate need of liberation from human degradation and oppression, a reality that was not felt by most of white American Christianity. As E. J. Carnell, one of white conservative evangelicalism's most well known theologians, once wrote,

---

8. Gayraud S. Wilmore, *Black Religion and Black Radicalism* (Garden City, N.Y.: Anchor Press/Doubleday, 1973), 10.

9. Edward P. and Anne S. Wimberly, *Liberation and Human Wholeness: The Conversion Experiences of Black People in Slavery and Freedom* (Nashville, Tenn.: Abingdon, 1986), 19–20.

> Too much stress on racial injustice will divert the sinner's attention
> from the need to repent of his totally self-centered life. . . . If we
> let the Negro buy a house in a fashionable suburb we do an injus-
> tice to vested property interests.[10]

That statement illustrates well the tendency of many wealthy Christians to dichotomize the "spiritual" from the "social" dimensions of the gospel, thereby capitulating to institutional structures which maintain their privileged position in the social hierarchy. African Americans have learned to be suspicious when white Christians talk much about the "soul" but rarely about the "body," when mysticism gets divorced from propheticism. Such dichotomies are foreign to their African-rooted spiritual experience.

The most distinguished figure in the black mystical tradition is Howard Thurman, who died in 1981 after a distinguished career in ministry and in academia. He was raised in poverty in rural Florida, nurtured in the black church, and received financial assistance to attend Morehouse College and Colgate Rochester Theological Seminary, graduating in 1926. After pastoring in Oberlin, Ohio, for two years, Thurman left for Haverford College to study with the Quaker philosopher and mystical writer Rufus Jones. He was especially influenced by the writings of the mystic Meister Eckhart and, later, St. Francis of Assisi. His career would lead him to a preaching and teaching ministry at Morehouse College, Howard University, the Church for the Fellowship of All Peoples in San Francisco, and Boston University.

Thurman authored over twenty books, numerous articles, and many interviews, addresses, and sermons. The titles of his books reflect his mystical leanings, such as *The Centering Moment, Deep is the Hunger, Disciplines of the Spirit, The Inward Journey, The Luminous Darkness,* and *Meditations of the Heart.*

Throughout his career, Howard Thurman touched an ever-widening circle of people across racial, social, religious, and national lines, yet always he acknowledged his African-American

---

10. E. J. Carnell, *The Case for Biblical Christianity*, ed. Ronald Nash (Grand Rapids, Mich.: Eerdmans Publishing Co., 1969), 90–91.

spiritual heritage to be the starting point for his mystical theology. In his autobiography, Thurman recalled an encounter with one of his white academic advisors who urged him to forget about dealing with racial concerns in his ministry:

> "You are a very sensitive Negro man," he said, "and doubtless feel under great obligation to put all of the weight of your mind and spirit at the disposal of the struggle of your people for full citizenship. But let me remind you that all social questions are transitory in nature and it would be a terrible waste for you to limit your creative energy to the solution of the race problem. Give yourself to the timeless issues of the human spirit," he advised. . . . I pondered the meaning of his words, and wondered what kind of response I could make to this man who did not know that a man *and his black skin* must face the "timeless issues of the human spirit" together.[11]

Later, when Thurman was invited to deliver the prestigious Ingersol Lectures at Harvard Divinity School in 1946, he was eager to introduce his scholarly audience to the religious genius of his African-American forebears. He believed that "the indigenous insights inherent in the Negro spirituals bear significantly on the timeless search for the meaning of life and death in human experience."[12] The lectures were published in his volume *Deep River: An Interpretation of Negro Spirituals*. The core message of the lectures was that the spirituals demonstrate the capability of the human spirit to make meaning of one's past, present, and future in the hereafter. In the spirituals, the slave singers were proclaiming that in the face of all evidence to the contrary, life was still worth living.

Thurman's life and thought maintained the balance between the spiritual and the social that is the hallmark of African-American spirituality. His method, however, of seeking societal transformation through the process of transforming individuals did not lend itself to becoming a leader of social justice movements, although he applauded that work. He once said of

---

11. Howard Thurman, *With Head and Heart: The Autobiography of Howard Thurman* (New York: Harcourt Brace Jovanovich, 1979), 60.

12. Ibid., 217.

himself, "I have never considered myself any kind of leader. . . .
I'm not a movement man. It's not my way. I work at giving witness in the external aspect of my life to my experience of the
truth. That's my way—the way the grain in my wood moves."[13]

In his book *The Creative Encounter,* Thurman writes of four
movements of the spiritual life, each entitling a chapter: "The
Inwardness of Religion," "The Outwardness of Religion," "The
Inner Need for Love," and "The Outer Necessity for Love." He
summarizes his reflections by calling for a harmonizing of these
movements in actual experience. In his vision for society, Thurman
sees the individual functioning in such a way that "the dichotomy
that exists between his professional life and his private life, between
his formal life and his informal life, between his inner life and his
outer life, must be reduced steadily to the vanishing point."[14]

Conclusion

THE TITLE OF this essay is taken from an old black spiritual:

> Oh, freedom! Oh, freedom! Oh, freedom over me!
> An' be fo' I'd be a slave, I'll be buried in my grave
> An' go home to my Lord an' be free.

At first glance, the sense of the spiritual may be thought to
be only escapist and compensatory, looking forward to the release
that the grave will bring from the troubles of this world with the
hope of a future reward. The mystical vision of heaven as a place
with "No mo' moanin', No mo' weepin'," and where "There'll be
singin'" is contrasted sharply with the reality that one is a slave in
this world. One longs to be in heaven, but in the meantime med-
itates on its joys day and night as a means of escape from the
hopeless situation of the moment.

But such docility never took a stronghold in African-
American spirituality, much to the consternation of the white

---

13. Lerone Bennett, Jr., "Howard Thurman: Twentieth-Century Holy
Man," *Ebony* 33 (February 1977).

14. Howard Thurman, *The Creative Encounter* (New York: Harper and
Brothers, 1954), 131.

slaveholders who thought that the introduction of Christianity would make the Africans better slaves, more accepting of their lot in life. Instead, the rapturous visions of and messages from heaven empowered the slaves to defy the status quo even more by any means they had at their disposal. The mystic impulse gave the impetus for prophetic action. The black church *led* the struggle for freedom in America *because* it had learned to listen for the liberating voice of God amidst the competing human voices clamoring to be heard. Those voices did not speak the way of God. The African knew that freedom, both personal and social, was God's intention for the world, and that slavery must always be opposed even if that opposition met with death: "An' be fo' I'd be a slave, I'll be buried in my grave, an' go home to my Lord an' be free!"

Our African forebears knew that the Lord God delivers those who are oppressed to freedom, as typified by the liberation of God's people from slavery in Egypt. But they also knew that this same God was *within* them as well, freeing them from personal bondage to freedom in Christ, leading them on a spiritual journey to Divine union. Christian mysticism has its roots in African soil and deep within the African soul, from the writings of the early Desert Fathers and Mothers, the flowering of contemplative spirituality in North Africa, to the origins of the Christian monasticism in Egypt represented by such figures as Antony and Pachomius. The Christian contemplative heritage began in Africa and continues to be nurtured by the descendants of Africa in diaspora around the world.

Centering Prayer is a way for African Americans to connect again with their spiritual roots. Contemplation recalls the deep river of knowing God that flows from Africa, connecting with all in the human family who seek God in silence as well as in activity. When I sit to pray, I am firmly in the tradition not only of the ancient Christians, many of whom were African, but also my African-American fathers and mothers of the faith who meditated on a God who loved them, uplifted them and empowered them to live when living seemed hopeless. God then sent them into the world on a mission: to proclaim and to do God's will on earth as it is in heaven.

Nurtured on the ecstatic fervor of worship in the black church and spurred to follow Christ where he is found among the poor and the oppressed of the world, it is natural that I should also be drawn to the silence of God, that I might consent to the divine presence and action in my own life. It is the way of African-American spirituality, and it is a way for us all.

6 🕸

The Art of Dialogue and Centering Prayer

Kay Lindahl

Centering Prayer is a prayer of the heart. Dialogue is a conversation of the heart.

I was introduced to Centering Prayer as a participant in a workshop titled "Making a Difference: A Course for Those Who Minister," sponsored by the Mastery Foundation and presented by one of its founders, Father Basil Pennington. Fr. Basil is one of the Trappist monks who distilled Centering Prayer from the ancient Christian contemplative tradition. Centering Prayer immediately became a regular, daily practice as I recognized that I had long been seeking this mode of silent prayer, which could lead me to the very center of my being in God. I had come home.

At the same time, I was deeply involved in the creation of the Alliance for Spiritual Community, an interfaith organization. In working on mission and vision statements, we discovered that one vital way of supporting inter-religious understanding and respect was to have monthly gatherings just to talk about what we personally believed, what was held in common between traditions, and what their peculiarities were. These were not so much lectures or debates about religious and sacred traditions as they were opportunities for personal sharing.

Each month we would consider a topic, such as community, friendship, or family, and listen to beliefs and practices of persons from various traditions. One person would be designated the facilitator. We adopted a few simple guidelines to enhance our ability to listen to disparate points of view and belief systems. While the guidelines were a vessel, a rich space for personal sharing, these offerings in turn shaped the guidelines. We had spontaneously come upon an experiential realization that these sharings were not only a key, but also a necessity to fully express what we believed. In simpler terms, there is only so much self-exploration that one can do on one's own.

During this time, a friend introduced me to the work of Dr. David Bohm, the noted physicist, whose interest in the nature of thought and communication led him to hypothesize that the basis of culture and society is shared meaning, a social construction of truth. He posits that meaning exists on a pre-conscious level and that the only way to articulate and examine these underpinnings is a through a process of dialogue, which would allow the shared meaning to emerge from a group or culture.

The Dialogue Process

ADOPTING A DIALOGUE process begins with an understanding of its nature. Dialogue is derived the Greek word *dialogos*. (*Logos* means "the word" or "essence of the word" and *dia* means "through.") Dialogue can be envisioned as a stream of meaning flowing through and among us, out of which will emerge some new understanding that initially was not individually present: a shared meaning. Dialogue encourages deep levels of listening and reflection, of being present to others. It is an inquiry, a wanting to know, a curiosity about others, and a developing of a sense of appreciation for differing points of view. It leads to an opening of the heart.

We contrast dialogue with the word *discussion,* which comes from the Latin *dis* (which means "apart") and *quatere* (which means "to shake"), the same root shared by percussion and concussion. A discussion can be considered a way of breaking things up to dissect and analyze their differences. Discussion is often characterized by each person presenting a different point of view and trying to convince others to agree with his or her view. Often, there is a focus on results, a win-lose outcome, with its accompanying sense of competition.

Certainly, there is nothing wrong with discussion. It is not only a valid way of communicating and producing results, but it is also an important element of creative tension. Normal conversation moves back and forth between dialogue and discussion without making distinctions between the two. Somehow we manage to communicate with each other. However, being aware of this distinction can make an extraordinary difference in how we relate to one another and how we can deepen our relationships.

It is particularly useful to recognize if you are in a discussion or a dialogue when you are dealing with emotionally charged topics. One reliable trait that identifies discussion experientially is that each person has an agenda, with facts or anecdotal information to argue his or her point of view. One listens to find weaknesses and rebuttals to the other's argument, rather than listening to gain comprehension. In discussion, one is more often looking for differences than for common ground. Dialogue is more often characterized by listening to understand the other, looking for threads of commonality, seeking some new insight about the subject that the participants had not considered before. Agreement is not necessary because the conversation does not hinge on winning and losing, convincing and being convinced. Meaningful conversation is intuitively sensed as a means of connecting with another in a new or deepening relationship.

As in Centering Prayer, dialogue calls for a deep level of receptivity and listening. The art of listening—being fully present with another—takes time and patience. So does the art of listening to one's true self, which is the fruit of the practice of Centering Prayer. In dialogue, it is all too easy to come up with an instant response. We are oriented towards results. However, listening happens when we stop speaking (thinking, figuring it out, preparing responses) and when we hope or consciously intend to hear something we do not already know. In dialogue, as in Centering Prayer, the role of intention is essential.

Once I started practicing a dialogue process, I felt that I had found a way to my center while being in community. Dialogue became a practice that strengthens my ability to connect with others, as much as Centering Prayer strengthens my ability to connect with God.

Dialogue in Centering Prayer Groups

As I became more familiar with Contemplative Outreach's network of Centering Prayer Groups, I appreciated the advantage of mutual support through sharing with other contemplatives the experience of Centering Prayer and its fruits in daily life. A typical Centering Prayer group has a format of experience (a prayer period), education (an on-going exploration of the conceptual background to the Contemplative dimension of the Gospel through books and tapes), and a period of sharing. Contemplative Outreach recommends that the sharing be centered on personal experience of the prayer and its fruits in daily life rather than on issues of formal theology or philosophy.

Most often, such groups are facilitated by a member of the Centering Prayer group. Many report that it is sometimes challenging to keep the sharing focused on personal experience and listening (dialogue) and discourage it from straying into discussions of theology and philosophy.

As I began to reflect further on the practice of dialogue, I realized that it is in many ways parallel to the process of Centering Prayer. Each has intention, guidelines, and fruits in everyday life. In exploring these aspects, I began to see how one practice truly complements the other, particularly in Centering Prayer groups.

Intention in Dialogue

Both Basil Pennington and Thomas Keating emphasize that intention is everything in Centering Prayer. Though it is a method, its "results" do not depend on how well you do it, but on why you do it. The intention of Centering Prayer is to deepen one's personal relationship with God, the ground of our being, beyond thoughts, feelings, and words. A primary intention of the dialogue process is to deepen one's relationship to others. A method of dialogue is not what yields the connection, but the intention of the participants to go beyond any one person's individual understanding to arrive at new insights that could not have been achieved individually. The core intention of dialogue, particularly in Centering Prayer groups, is the creation and support of spiritual community. Just as individual understanding can blossom into common understanding of our relationship with God, so too can such dialogue affirm the spiritual nature of all communities. This relaxes not only individual but communal tensions. Understanding opens through a chain reaction: the more we understand about one another, the less we fear; hence the more we risk and the more we trust, which opens our hearts to one another in love.

One recent example I witnessed of the impact of intention in dialogue occurred at a small interfaith gathering which included Christians and two Buddhists. At one point, we paired off for an exercise in dialogue, and one of the Buddhists was partnered with a Pentecostal Christian, who later reported that originally he was uneasy about the Buddhists even being in the group. As a committed Christian, he wasn't sure how he would he be able to relate to non-Christians, even though they might be as committed as he was to their own faith tradition. He was initially tempted to begin a conversion discussion, potentially one of the most emotionally charged type of win-lose conversations, to bring the Buddhist to his belief in Christ. Luckily, he remembered the guidelines of the dialogue, particularly the intention of learning something new about someone else, and he realized that it was not an appropriate time to proselytize. By the end of the dialogue exercise, he discovered that he and his Buddhist partner were about as far apart as they could be in their beliefs, but that they were totally aligned in their values. He called the Buddhist his brother. They left the gathering feeling related to each other in spirit.

Shared intention deepens our relationships and creates a context, or vessel, for dialogue. The intention to listen and learn something new about someone implies good will. We enter into a dialogue process with a larger purpose in mind. It is similar to the individual intention of Centering Prayer in which we consent to God's presence and action within ourselves. In dialogue, we have the intention to consent to God's presence and action within others and within the group as a whole.

Guidelines

CENTERING PRAYER IS taught in terms of guidelines, not "do's" and "don'ts." The core guideline is to introduce the sacred word, the prayer word, inwardly and to gently return to it whenever we find our mind or heart is elsewhere. The sacred word becomes a symbol of our intention to consent to God's presence and action within us. There is an element of freedom, a letting go, and then when we find ourselves thinking any other thought, there is the gentle reassertion of our intention. Similarly, a method of dialogue can be seen as the freedom of sharing our deeper feelings and beliefs in a safe environment, and when we recognize that we have moved beyond, to reassert our intention to seek God's presence and action within each other and the group.

Since the distinction between dialogue and discussion is often overlooked, a few simple guidelines to support the dialogue process are offered. They are certainly useful in the sharing period of a Centering Prayer group, as well as in an independent dialogue process which might explore a particular issue or topic:

1. Suspend assumptions.
2. Listen and speak without judgment.
3. Express your personal response.
4. Focus on inquiry and reflection.
5. Suspend status.
6. Maintain confidentiality.
7. Listen for understanding.

It might be helpful to briefly consider the essence of each guideline.

Suspend Assumptions

ASSUMPTIONS ARE USUALLY transparent: We often are unaware that we have them or that they motivate our conversation. Yet assumptions prevent us from truly understanding each other. We automatically assume that others have had the same experiences that we have had. Dialogue—listening to understand—reveals that each of us has had different experiences in life which we bring to our conversations. Simply put, we all look at life from different perspectives, and leaving our own particular assumptions aside greatly facilitates the listening process.

One clue to self-awareness of assumptions is to try to notice when one of our "hot buttons" is being pushed by something someone else has said. Commentaries we think to ourselves are the clearest sign of assumptions. "How can he or she say such a thing? That's the dumbest thing I ever heard!" Sometimes our response may appear in emotions such as anger, fear, or discomfort at what someone has said. If there is uneasiness, usually there is an assumption hiding out. Often we assume the other person means something completely different from what he or she actually intend, and it is our assumption that makes us deaf. Thomas Keating calls these afflictive emotions a "map of the false self."

When we feel an afflictive emotion, it is often an appropriate time to ask a clarifying question with the intent to understand, not to challenge, fix, or convince. The best way to deal with assumptions is to notice them, express them if it would clear the air, and then put them aside so we can really listen to what someone else is saying. The fruits of the dialogue process will help dissipate the very assumptions that might otherwise limit the process.

Listen and Speak without Judgment

THIS GUIDELINE IS a real challenge because we, as human beings, must learn to judge and evaluate in order to make decisions which guide our daily life. Judgment reveals itself in our inner conversation with our feelings: "I like this, I don't like that; this is good, that is bad; this is right, that is wrong." Such commentaries are more often emotional than rational. They are also cumulative, as present decisions are often based on past decisions. Judgments happen in an instant and most often arise from habit: we are not usually conscious that we have made a judgment about someone or something. In a dialogue, we are interested in being open to new understandings and perspectives. Suspending our judgments when we sense them can create a space between having a reaction and expressing it, which in turn allows us to listen to another's point of view.

One aid to gaining awareness of our judgments is noticing our responses. When we find ourselves in disagreement, discomfort, or even in perfect, absolute agreement, we likely have made a judgment. It is the letting go of judgment which opens the door for new, shared meaning.

These movements in the first two dialogue guidelines are very similar to the letting go of thought and emotion in Centering Prayer and returning ever so gently to the sacred word. The habit of letting go that develops with a regular practice of Centering Prayer can't help but carry over into daily life, freeing us more and more from assumptions and judgments in dealing with others. Like thoughts and emotions during Centering Prayer, the more we accept that assumptions and judgments are present in our psyche, the less we are ruled by them. Whenever we become aware we are off on the tangents of assumptions and judgments, it is recommend that we simply return to being mindfully present in the dialogue. This returning to what the other person is saying is much akin to the reassertion of our intention in Centering Prayer by returning to the sacred word.

Express Your Personal Response

EACH PERSON SHOULD speak for him or herself, keeping his or her reaction connected to his or her own personal experience. Another way to say this is to watch the pronouns we use. Speaking in the first person singular, using "I" language, almost requires us to speak from our own experience, from our hearts. However, speaking in the first person plural, using "we" and "you" pronouns in dialogue, often sounds as if we assume something is so for everyone in the room. It also starts to sound preachy. Most often, using "we" and "you" keeps us speaking from the head rather than the heart.

Other ways that we slip away from personal response into assumptions and judgments is in using phrases such as "we all know," "of course," "everyone knows," "most people," and "all of us." Another pitfall is to respond with a "you should." Dialogue provides an opportunity to listen without having to do or fix anything.

Focus on Inquiry and Reflection

THE GOAL OF dialogue is not to find answers but to be in the question. We develop a sense of wonder and curiosity about what another person thinks. We practice listening simply to see what will emerge next, rather than what we think should be said. There is a wonderful Quaker maxim expressing this point: "It's a sin to speak when you're not moved to speak. It's a sin not to speak when you're moved to speak."

This guideline points to the importance of silence and reflection in dialogue. To allow a participant or the group to pause in the conversation if necessary can renew the ability to listen mindfully and to renew the intention of being present to God's presence and action within the group. Pausing in a conversation and letting the silence speak is almost counter-cultural in our society. Notice how quickly someone starts talking when there is a lull in a conversation. It's as though silence is a dreaded vacuum that forces speaking. However, if we can allow silence to be part of the dialogue, the thinking process will slow down, and we will take time to reflect and open up to the possibility of a new understanding. This is very similar to the process of Centering Prayer, which thinking and feeling slow down and we eventually become centered in the silence.

If you are in a Centering Prayer group and the sharing dialogue follows the period of prayer, the silence of the prayer will naturally be an element of the conversation. If you are in a dialogue process for other purposes, ten minutes of Centering Prayer prior to starting the dialogue is highly recommended to establish reflection and silence.

Suspend Status

EVERYONE IS AN equal partner in a dialogue. There are no senior or junior participants because we are all experts in our own life experience. One person's offering is just as valid as the next person's. There is no place in a dialogue for authority or hierarchy. Acting in a spirit of respectful equality requires trust in each other and in the process so that we can be open without feeling unnecessarily vulnerable. One sign that a dialogue is happening is when you feel that you can express yourself even though it is not a popular or even commonly held thought, conviction, or feeling.

Maintain Confidentiality

EACH PARTICIPANT, INDEED the group as a whole, should agree never to attach the names of the other participants to what they have expressed. It is natural to want to share, particularly with others outside the dialogue, the enthusiasm arising from a deepening relationship or a helpful insight occurring through dialogue. Indeed, sharing outside the dialogue is a way of integrating such transformative opportunities into our daily life. A group should safely welcome the sharing of stories and ideas that emerge from the dialogue. However, to preserve the trust in the group process, it is recommend that the name of the participant not be identified or attached to the story or expression. We do this to create a safe space for people to express themselves fully without a concern that what they say will be taken out of context or create embarrassment. Sometimes dialogue participants will give permission to use their name. Even then it is advisable to exercise discretion, if only for the sake of the group and its integrity. Confidentiality provides freedom to explore and express insights and new perspectives. Thomas Keating and Basil Pennington both teach that intimacy and friendship naturally give rise to self-disclosure, which in turn deepens our relationships with God and others.

Listen for Understanding

WHEN WE LISTEN for understanding, it is not necessary to reach agreement, to concur, or to ratify, though they are all valid tools in discussions. Often, in dialogue we find that we do not agree with anything that is said. If this is an accepted dimension of the dialogue, one is frequently surprised that even this inability to agree becomes part of a shared meaning, emerging beyond each other's assumptions. We sometimes have to be consciously aware that there is no need for an answer, solution, or result in a dialogue. Our intention is to hear what the others are saying. This most often leads to a warming of the heart, an opening of the mind, and the capacity to hear diverse opinions and points of view. It is a profound experience to realize that someone else's beliefs are as meaningful to them as ours are to us. It does not mean that we have to abandon our beliefs and convictions and accept each other's beliefs to achieve harmony or understanding. As in music, different notes often achieve harmony, counterpoint, and even at times a pleasent dissonance.

Dialogue is a living process of releasing, letting go, and accepting what comes. It is a continual opportunity for learning and understanding, for being mindfully present in the moment, for speaking from the heart, and for allowing new possibilities in communication and community building to emerge.

The Fruits of Dialogue

JUST AS THOSE who have a regular practice of Centering Prayer best measure its worth by its fruits in their own lives, so too participants in a dialogue process can look to its effect in their daily life. Often dialogue participants begin to listen more openly in everyday conversations and interactions. It is commonly reported that relationships outside the dialogue group experience improvement, particularly in intimate relationships, which are often the most accessible but the hardest to renew. With a spouse, partner, child, or parent, listening to understand, not to agree or disagree, leads to the common ground of shared meaning where the relationship can accommodate differences and still thrive.

Another commonly reported fruit of dialogue is that one abandons the instinct or need to make others into our idea of who they should be. Instead we come to appreciate others for being who they really are, opening up an ever-present but sometimes obscure reality.

Many simply report that the dialogue space creates a sacred, holy ground on which to understand and appreciate their role in other people's lives.

In my life, the influence of this process is pervasive. I more easily notice when a conversation becomes competitive (my side versus another's side) before issues have been fully explored and common ground discovered. I also find that because I am more present in conversation, I hear things that I wouldn't have heard otherwise. I have more compassion and respect for others, particularly those unlike myself. By establishing such a connection, I feel more connected to others in my life beyond the dialogue. As a result, I believe others open up to me in a new way. I am aware especially that this is an ongoing practice.

The practice of Centering Prayer is an exercise for my spiritual well being. The practice of dialogue is an exercise for both my inter-personal and community well being. Both are healing, both impact my relationships, both open my heart. In both, there is no need to hurry, no goal to achieve, just love to share.

Dialogue is to love what blood is to the body.
When the flow of blood stops, the body dies.
When dialogue stops, love dies and resentment and hate are born.
But dialogue can restore a dead relationship.
Indeed, this is the miracle of dialogue:
It can bring relationships into being, and
It can bring into being once again a relationship that has died.

There is only one qualification to these claims for dialogue:
It must be mutual and proceed from both sides, and
The parties to it must persist relentlessly.

7 ✺

"Where Two or Three Are Gathered": Centering Prayer and the Small Group Process

LYLA YASTION

Upon returning from the rarefied atmosphere of a Centering Prayer ten-day intensive at Snowmass, Colorado, in May 1996, I experienced a renewed enthusiasm, not only for the art of Centering Prayer, which I had been practicing since reconverting to Catholicism after a twenty year immersion in Eastern mantra meditation, but also for the doctoral project in anthropology which I was about to tackle. What had clarified in my mind out in the snow-capped expanse of Colorado, which cradled the retreat community's consent to a deepening of the contemplative practice, was the focus of the dissertation: an examination of the dynamic interplay (which I had just experienced) between individual spiritual development through Centering Prayer and the group process supporting that practice known as Contemplative Outreach (CO). I saw immediately that this focus was itself wrapped in a context which could not be ignored: I had to decipher CO's persona, both as a contemporary socioreligious movement arising out of the experimentation that followed Vatican II reforms and as a group phenomenon embedded in the fabric of American cultural history. I knew I would bump up against the perennial scholarly debate as to how much and when America's intense individualism permitted communal consciousness—but more of that later.

It wasn't until the following January, after most of my course work was out of the way, that I decided on the fieldwork site. I would limit my research to seven of the twenty Centering Prayer groups in the New York metropolitan area (i.e., seven of the eight Manhattan groups), attending their weekly meetings regularly for a twelve-month period to familiarize myself at some depth with their operation, while also requesting permission to attend any major conferences and training seminars offered by CO during that time span.

I was invited to attend a "business" meeting that January held at a Manhattan Roman Catholic church. Any interested CO practitioners in the area were welcome. The meeting was led by Gail Fitzpatrick-Hopler, Executive Director of CO and Doris Curley, then the New York City CO coordinator. The purpose of the dialogue was to consider the "New York problem": why were the Centering Prayer support groups not more numerous and robust in growth in New York City as they were in other key areas of, for example, Colorado and Florida? What might be done to support these existing groups in order to give a jump start to Father Keating's hometown? The brainstorming of the twenty-five participants produced some creative suggestions, such as a Formation Training—for those interested in accelerating their own spiritual development while increasing their understanding of CO group process—in which time-scheduling would be tailored to meet people's often harried work and family obligations. The conversation also highlighted obstacles about which I had been reading—those "American" problems tackled since the 1960s by prominent social scientists and historians, obstacles which may be particularly endemic to big cities.

One of these obstacles is a radical individualism which, according to Robert Bellah et al. in *Habits of the Heart*, has progressively eaten away at America's biblical and republican identifications that have historically bound the individual to the community through the practice of civic duty.[1] This deterioration has reduced religion to a phenomenon Bellah and his colleagues call "Sheilaism" after a woman who, when asked her religion, replied that she chose to fashion her religious beliefs after her own particular preferences. Christopher Lasch, in *The Culture of Narcissism*, argues that such an inward turn can easily become an act of narrow self-interest, a cultural trait which de Tocqueville, in his 1836 visit to the democratic America, admired for its myriad voluntary associations but he prophetically warned could destroy the nation if exaggerated.[2] It may be that the reported explosion of support groups—including CO—of varied kinds since the 1960s is a compensatory mechanism to restore a needed balance.[3] Even spirituality can be an insidious means to self-aggrandizement, a complement to individual material acquisitiveness. Thomas Keating warns that "the spiritual journey is not a success story or a career move. It is rather a series of humiliations of the false self."[4]

Another obstacle which was recognized at the New York meeting is the smorgasbord of spiritual options in the religious marketplace, not only in New York City but across America. The 1960s witnesses a reawakening of a slumbering and complacent

1. Robert N. Bellah, Richard Madsen, William M. Sullivan, Ann Swidler, and Steven M. Tipton, *Habits of the Heart: Individualism and Commitment in American Life* (New York: Harper and Row, 1985).

2. Christopher Lasch, *The Culture of Narcissism* (New York: W. W. Norton, 1979); Alexis de Tocqueville, *Democracy in America*, vol. 2 (New York: Alfred A. Knopf, 1980), 318.

3. Shaffer and Anundsen (1993) report a quadrupling of support groups between 1980–90 with fifteen million Americans attending five hundred thousand various support groups. In Carolyn R. Shaffer and Kristin Anundsen, *Creating Community Anywhere: Finding Support and Connection in a Fragmented World* (New York: Putnam Publishing Group, 1993), 71.

4. Thomas Keating, *Intimacy with God* (New York: Crossroad, 1996), 85.

religiosity in America, which has had a life-long history of revivalist fervor unrivaled in any other Western nation.[5] How would a new spiritual offering, especially a low key, contemplative support network, compete with the panoply of religious and secular self-help options out there?

The motivating sound of inquiry at that meeting launched me into a grassroots examination of the seven Centering Prayer groups which met at various Roman Catholic churches dotted across the Manhattan landscape. Doris provided me with a current list of names and phone numbers. I got in touch with facilitators of the groups and received permission to participate in weekly meetings in the role of observer-participator. In staggered fashion, I would stay with each group four months. In addition, I signed up for the new five-month Saturday Formation Training in New York City and attended both the Lectio Divina Conference in Beech Grove, Indiana, that January and the Andover, Maryland, National CO Conference the following October. The latter ground-breaking conference introduced me to the politics of dialogue and consensus which led to the modification and ratification of the CO Vision Statement and Theological Principles. This document forms the heart of the young ten-year-old collective CO network. Both conferences provided a deeper understanding of CO's vision and mission within contemporary Catholic Christianity and beyond that to its open ecumenical participation.

It is the purpose of this article to present to the reader a microcosm of group process. Because the field site is of necessity circumscribed, it may not reflect with full accuracy larger regional or national characteristics; however, as a microcosm, these seven Manhattan centering groups may serve as a limb providing insights about the CO network as a whole body—as Keating maintains, an "organism," not an "organization" (Andover Conference, October 1997). I will limit this present analysis to: (1) a consideration of the development of unique "group personalities"; (2) variability in the structure of meetings; and (3) the

---

5. For a full treatment of America's revivalist heritage see Jon Butler, *Awash in a Sea of Faith* (Cambridge: Harvard University Press, 1990).

knotty issue of volunteerism and commitment to the group. I will allude periodically to characteristics which, at the risk of stereotypic categorization, appear to me to reflect facets of American culture, particularly those traits also harmonious with initial Vatican II democratic aspirations of which CO is representative. I will conclude with suggestions for further growth towards committed faith communities at the grassroots level. These suggestions reflect my impressions from observation and experience; they are thus inevitably subjective. A gift of postmodernist thinking—for all its extreme deconstructionist tactics—has been the recognition in social science research of the *illusion* of objectivity as well as the insight that, paraphrasing Paul Ricoeur, "one studies the other to know one's self."[6] This admission raises the spiritual question: can there be an "other" in reality?

Vagaries of Group Formation

IN APRIL I visited my first CO introductory workshop at an uptown parish followed by the formation there of a new Centering Prayer group. Fifteen people (three males, twelve females) attended the workshop. They were mostly parishioners who had heard about the workshop through an announcement in the parish bulletin or by word-of-mouth. A CO presenter well-schooled in presentation skills and likable because of his humble charm, gave out the basics to a receptive audience. A married couple volunteered to lead the new group, and a first meeting date was scheduled.

The first evening meeting was held in the beautiful church sanctuary which had been frequented by Thomas Merton during his Columbia University days. The parish priest was there; thereafter, he attended when he could. The atmosphere of setting and purpose could not have been more conducive. But where was the group? I had expected at least ten of the fifteen workshop participants to come. Including the two facilitators and myself, we numbered six. In the ensuing weeks, we gained one member and lost one; several newcomers attended off and on for a few

---

6. Paul Ricoeur, *From Text to Action: Essays in Hermeneutics II* (Evanston: Northwestern University Press, 1991), 17.

weeks. We eventually settled with a core of six (counting myself). Sometimes someone would show up with no idea of what Centering Prayer was and no time to receive proper instruction; one person would blend in, another would leave confused. It seemed happenstance. The facilitators, new themselves to their function, tried to accommodate people's needs, but the whole affair seemed clumsy and I began to doubt whether the group would hold together. When I voiced my dismay to the core members, they showed not the least perturbation. Numbers meant little; intention, devotion was all. Was I unnecessarily anxious? Had I forgotten Jesus' words, "Where two or three are gathered together in my name there am I in the midst of them"?[7] I realized I was suffering from the modern disease of overreliance on quantitative statistical judgments based on the myth of the righteousness of large numbers. Between the concept of *mass* and the other extreme of *alienating individualism* is the supportive *small group community* exemplifying our historic American heritage of voluntary associations. As a friend from another group confided to me some months later:

> I hate that number thing. If this were the case I wouldn't be in Contemplative Outreach. It's the Spirit working. It's beautiful. The group can be two; two's a group. This recruiting stuff is horrible.[8]

A September follow-up visit to the new group revealed a stable core of six members. Minor changes had come about in the format of the *lectio divina* and in seating arrangements in the sanctuary. The husband-facilitator told me that the participants had been greatly strengthened by the quiet presence of one member in particular, the magnificent setting, and the participatory support of the priest. Practicing with the members, I could feel a quiet grounding of shared intention. A group had formed.

As my visits to other groups ensued, I saw a similar pattern. With comings and goings of members uneven in their attendance, the steadiness of a small core held the group together.

---

7. Matthew 18:20.

8. This and all successive quotes from group members are recorded in dated fieldnotes during this twelve-month study.

The older the group, the more secure the membership: the core, with now and then a new person joining or visiting from another Centering Prayer group. A policy across the board was no canceling of meetings, though sometimes it was unclear, even among the core, who would come. Promptness was expected and materialized in most cases. My admiration grew for the stalwart few. As one core member said to me proudly, "We're a loyal bunch!" My annoyance grew as well, however, in regards to what appeared to be a lack of commitment by some individuals to their group, an attitude that said "I will come if I need it . . . if I have time," and an assumption that "Someone will be there. Someone always is." I had heard that several groups in Manhattan had folded for various reasons. Was lack of commitment one of them?

Group Composition

CO IS PRINCIPALLY a lay phenomenon, although its founder and a percentage of its membership have been drawn from religious orders as well as from the clergy of Catholic and other denominations, especially Episcopalian. In the seven groups studied the total number of participants—approximate because of the sporadic attendance of some—was fifty-three. The more reliable *core* member total was thirty-nine, with an average of five to six members attending each group per week. There were some special situations: two core members moved out of town during my tenure; one member, though she wished to come regularly, was handicapped and depended on assistance which was not always available; two core members participated in more than one group per week because, as one told me, "I like the immersion." As a rule, facilitators' attendance was regular; but in one case in which there were two facilitators, one rarely showed and the other had to rely on another member's dedicated regularity to assist when she could not come because of conflicting obligations. Dick Westley, in *Good Things Happen: Experiencing Community in Small Groups*, points out that every small Christian community, like the church, needs a *rock person* whose dedication—as Peter's—

sustains the group through thick and thin.[9] This group has just begun to stabilize in the last few months.

A majority of the participants were women (45:8), of which about 75 percent were single or widowed.[10] The average age range

---

9. Dick Westley, *Good Things Happen: Experiencing Community in Small Groups* (Mystic: Twenty-third Publications, 1992), 98.

10. Female/male ratio is a variable to be considered, but not at length here. Suffice it to say that CO representatives have concurred that there is a predominance of women in small support groups nation-wide, with more male representation at conferences (I observed a 3:1 ratio at the two conferences I attended). Reasons have been offered, the stereotypic reasons being "women are more devotional" and "women have more time." Yet to me, these answers are simplistic and may not even be accurate. For example, women's roles in the workplace have increased, giving them less time to attend religious or secular activities. There are also different types of *devotion*, the contemplative or mystic kind historically drawing men as well as women. Referring to a "feminization of the church" in the nineteenth century, Charles Morris in *American Catholic* (New York: Times Random House, 1997), 335 quotes a priest as saying women "have always been the heart of the Church" (Morris, *American Catholic*, 430).This may be so, but what does this "feminization" consist of? One answer may be that the predominantly lay Centering Prayer support groups provide an opportunity for close companionship and a relational communion of members with one another and with God. Studies such as Deborah Tannen's *You Just Don't Understand: Women and Men in Conversation* (New York: Morrow, 1990) have shown the ease and talent with which women approach such occasions of expressive dialogue and relational encounters. As facilitators and group members women can fully use these skills. Furthermore, the intuitive, loving journey of contemplative spirituality with its fruit of outward harmonious action may be not only natural to the female temperament but, up until recently, less explored by males because of a Western cultural bias. Theologian Ewert H. Cousins in *Christ of the Twenty-First Century* (Rockport: Element, 1992) and historian Richard Tarnas in *The Passion of the Western Mind: Understanding the Ideas That Have Shaped Our World View* (New York: Ballentine Books, 1991) have spoken of the need in this age for a tempering of the masculine aggressive perspective by the more feminine holistic, maternal, and relational approach. Whether one sees these latter traits as biologically or culturally conditioned—or both—does not change the fact that Western culture has been dominated since the Enlightenment by a rational (i.e., analytical, logical) separatist view of human being versus nature or the world, a view which steadily became manipulative and exploitative, invading the relationship between male and female to construct opposed dualities rather than complementaries to a union.

of participants was forty-five to seventy, with a predominance of Caucasian, well-educated (at least two years of college) professionals or professional retirees. Two of the women were nuns, and another woman, a facilitator, had spent some years in a seminary. Most participants had been brought up Catholic, but approximately a quarter said they had lapsed in their religious practice or had been exploring Eastern methods of meditation and had returned to Christianity under the aegis of Centering Prayer, which offered a much desired deep personal communion with God.

Because some of the selected groups had been together longer than others, I was afforded the opportunity to watch for signs of group development and change over time. Were there stages that one could anticipate, as is reported in literature on group dynamics? Of the seven, I designated three as *older* or *mature* (five to six years old), three as *young* (started in March and April 1997), and one as *adolescent* (one year old). This latter term is not meant to be pejorative but indicates rather accurately features I did not perceive at first: fluidity, enthusiasm, sociability, changeableness in number (for about a month ten to twelve people showed up, more than at any other group), and experimentation with format, especially with rotating facilitators which had its creative as well as awkward results.

Individual and Group

A GROUP IS a unit as concrete as an individual. Its life can nourish the individuals of which it is made and the society around it if it is conscious of itself as a whole body and if its motives are pure. In CO, the overriding motive is defined as "the intention to consent to God's will and action within" through the practice of Centering Prayer.[11] Jung argued that the process of individuation required small group interaction; witness even the dyad of therapist and patient.[12]

---

11. Thomas Keating, *Open Mind, Open Heart* (New York: The Continuum Publishing Company, 1995), 139.

12. Carl G. Jung, *Psychological Reflections* (New York: Harper and Brothers, 1953), 148.

The 1970s spiritual retrieval by Keating, Pennington, and Meninger offered Centering Prayer as an updated *individual* contemplative practice. However, it is instructive that this offering was seen to be incomplete until supplemented in the 1980s by the *group-oriented* network of Contemplative Outreach. Keating's background in monastic community along with his lay associate Gustave Reininger's experience with base ecclesial communities in Latin America were natural catalysts for the creative insights that launched this spiritual network system.

In social research, there are at present two opposing takes on the balance between individualism and group affiliations in American culture. Robert Wuthnow documents a current plethora of both secular and spiritual support groups.[13] It seems that the day of the rugged individual pulling up his or her own bootstraps survives only in the movies. Charles Morris reports that in Catholic churches the laity as "People of God" have become much more involved in revitalizing their parish, their community, and their own spirituality since Vatican II.[14] This participatory attitude is witnessed in such experiments as the Charismatic Renewal, RCIA, and Contemplative Outreach. According to Westley, there has been an upsurge in small Christian communities in the past thirty years. He argues that the community is born of the Holy Spirit and, therefore, is more a *becoming* than a *how-to exercise*; it requires loyal commitment to overweigh individual choice.[15] Through a gradual attrition of ego, "our deepest communal self" emerges to produce true community.[16] The "dream of Yahweh" is a joint enterprise at the grassroots level in which the church *is* a group of small communities rather than an institution to which, in fact, these communities give form and spiritual substance.[17]

13. Robert Wuthnow, *Sharing the Journey: Support Groups and America's New Quest for Community* (New York: The Free Press, 1994).

14. Morris, *American Catholic*, 320.

15. Westley, *Good Things Happen*, 9, 15.

16. Ibid., 41. This emergence corresponds to Peck's *mystical-communal* stage of group development described in M. Scott Peck, *The Different Drum: Community-Making and Peace* (New York: Simon and Schuster, 1987).

17. Ibid., 62.

On the other hand, Harvard professor Robert Putnam sees a diminishment in the legendary attraction of Americans for voluntary associations. His investigation of contributing factors finally designates television as major culprit because it encourages individual isolation and passivity.[18] More pessimistic is Harold Bloom's biting assessment of what he calls the "gnostic American Religion," which is focused on the individual's obsessive mystic quest for self unattached to any other self. He concludes that America is irretrievably and banefully individualistic.[19]

Although Bellah et al. also decry what their interviews with ordinary people show as excessive individualism, they propose a hopeful solution: the individual cultivation of mysticism and/or methods of contemplation to heighten consciousness. If this practice occurs *in numbers large enough to reach a critical mass,* individuals will be prompted to care for the larger social body. Or, to take Richard Neuhaus's metaphor, to bring the *sacred* back into the "naked public square."[20]

It is interesting that raising the level of consciousness in society has always been central to an authentic mystic journey, whatever the religious tradition. Evelyn Underhill, in her classic, *Mysticism,* states that true mystic experience translates into actions of group solidarity and compassion.[21] Resonating with this tradition Keating speaks of Centering Prayer as eliciting the fruits of the Spirit, particularly a bonding between group members which "gives us an inner desire to form community and to be faithful to it."[22] This sense of unity extends for "we become one with everything that

---

18. Robert D. Putnam "Tuning In, Tuning Out: the Strange Disappearance of Social Capital in America," *Political Science and Politics* 28:4 (1995), 664–83.

19. Harold Bloom, *The American Religion* (New York: Touchstone, 1992).

20. Bellah et al., *Habits of the Heart,* 286. Richard Neuhaus, *The Naked Public Square: Religion and Democracy in America* (Grand Rapids, Mich.: W. B. Eerdsman Publishing, 1984).

21. Evelyn Underhill, *Mysticism* (New York: Penguin Books, 1974) 174.

22. Keating, *Intimacy with God,* 158.

God has created."[23] Experience of intimacy with God imprints one's actions, manifesting an intimacy with Creation.

St. Paul's description in Romans 12 of the Body of Christ as composed of individuals with their several gifts elucidates the fact that neither the individual nor the social unit can be considered primary. The either-or approach betrays the linearity Western causal thinking. More open-ended and creative are the concepts of simultaneity, synchronicity, and dynamic animated flow between the individual and society—rather like the discovery in new physics of the "particle" as a particle or a wave depending on the environment. As late nineteenth-century American idealist philosopher Josiah Royce aptly put it: "Genuine individuality can be realized only through loyalty to the community, [for] self-knowledge is possible only in a social interactive context . . . others help me to interpret myself to myself."[24] Indeed, a group is not just a means of support to individual development but a *being* or *organism* in its own right, developing by its own laws.[25]

Group Process

WHEN KEATING ARGUED at the Andover conference that it was important to view CO as an "organism" rather than an "organization," he was differentiating between substance and form, between the live growth and evolution of group processes and mechanistic structures which can inhibit creative growth. The heart of both group and individual spiritual growth—that which enlivens it—is Centering Prayer. In the group meeting, this *task* is paramount. *Structural* components of setting and format surround the practice and can enhance it. Through Centering Prayer, the group can bond; this is *process*. In studying the seven Centering Prayer groups, I needed to examine *process* and *structure*, both seen through the lens of the *task*.

---

23. Ibid., 158.
24. In Frederick Charles Copleston, *A History of Philosophy,* vol. 8 (New York: Doubleday, 1994), 282.
25. For further insight on this important concept see Westley, *Good Things Happen*, 41.

Although I came in at different moments of each group's life during my twelve-month study, I became aware that I was witnessing an evolution, a dynamic of development in which—unconsciously it would appear—each group was forming itself as a "being" with a "personality." A precept of Centering Prayer is that the subtle working of the Holy Spirit guides the development of individual and group. Indeed, as I was reminded often by group members who were reminding themselves at moments of discouragement about their practice or their lives, it is the Holy Spirit who is "boss." We just need to get out of the way. And who is "we?" Keating would say the false self with its desires and agendas; let it go, pay it no mind; it will die of starvation.

I observed, therefore, that the underlying constant in all the groups—the essence or the soul of the group, as it were—was a tireless inner commitment, particularly of core members, to a receptive, God-directed waiting through the vehicle of Centering Prayer and a hope that the indwelling Holy Spirit who prays for us, as St. Paul says, is active and is moving us toward intimate relationship.

Some members intimated that progress in their own spiritual journey was linked to the group's life as a *body of Christ*. Here are some revealing comments recorded from informal conversations and from a response form which thirty-nine out of fifty-three group members returned to me. Their evaluations of group life show both the task-oriented benefits of group practice and the process-oriented or relational benefits. Most importantly, they reveal the *connection* between task and process [members' words in italics]:

TASK-ORIENTED: The group *inspires, encourages, renews, reminds, authenticates, helps me be faithful to,* fosters *commitment to, perseverance* and *consistency* in the practice, heightens *stillness, peace, relaxation, opens me up*; provides *enhanced religion, deep spirituality.*

PROCESS-ORIENTED: The group provides an opportunity to *share faith, goals, interpretations and insights* [re: lectio, centering practice] *with like-minded loving, warm people* who *become social and spiritual friends*; gives *courage to speak* and *be free in expression, spontaneous*; creates *good company, community, family, role models, mutual*

> aid in and outside of group setting, support in dry peri-
> ods and difficult life trials, bonded fellowship, increased
> accountability to self and group, loving uncritical sup-
> port, extends parish life in a meaningful way. The
> group *fulfills a need for true communication, exposure
> to God's creativity working in different people*, counters
> the isolation of prayer, teaches trust.

A number of comments addressed the importance in individual spiritual development of the evolution of group into community. Here are a few:

> I need others to complete myself spiritually . . . there is a stronger
> feeling of prayer when we are together . . . I only know myself
> through others, I cannot love God in a vacuum; God is palpable in
> a group of committed people. . . . As the individual's inherent
> value is apparent to the group so the value of group becomes
> apparent to the individual; where two or three are gathered the
> Lord is present in a special, more enhanced way and heightens a
> community spirit . . . a community bonded together in God's name
> can only be filled with His presence and graces . . . Jesus taught
> that religion is not between "God and me" but more "other"-
> oriented; He wants us to be in community.

As groups persevered together in weekly meetings, I
observed that the motivation for being there strengthened
enough in some people (i.e., the core) to effect a change in the
group dynamic, rather like changing gears in a car. One mature
group had been together five years. It met in a small office adjacent to a ground-floor chapel beneath which sounded the rumble
of racing subways. When I entered this group's world, I experienced a palpable, relaxed silence in which the members felt so
comfortable that they could extend it like a thread between format activities. The worldly hurriedness of time vanished during
the meeting and reappeared only on leaving the chapel.

Another group, which had met for six years in a parish which
housed many community and church activities, had started with
nine members, diminished to six and then dropped to three core
members at the time of my visits. The members accepted the fact
that not only had their numbers been reduced but that various
family, work, and transportation factors made it difficult for all

three to meet together every week; yet, they trusted each other's commitment to the group. One evening, when we all chanced to appear, the sanctuary was available for practice. I experienced the processional reverence of the meditative walk which this group inserted both before and between the two twenty minute centering practices and felt the quiet, subtle bonding which joined the members to each other during the prayer activities and even afterwards when the three embraced and talked for awhile.

It is clear from members' comments quoted above that a majority of individuals in all the groups recognized the importance of cultivating a group bonding built on faith in the practice and simple friendship. "I feel guilty now if I don't practice during the week," said one woman, and another in the same group said, in sudden illumination during *lectio divina*, "I'm grateful for the community here. Thank you, Lord." This group—one of the younger, larger groups—extends their friendships into socializing activities which are facilitated by the fact that five members live near each other. In other groups, such as the previously mentioned mature group, the bonding plays out in the enclosure of the group meeting only.

As people become more comfortable with each other and especially when a few have the courage to open themselves up in faith-sharing (if faith-sharing is encouraged by the facilitator, and this was highly variable in the groups I visited), there is a marked deepening of the group identity. In sharing personal experience regarding the centering practice as it affects one's life, both the individual and the group are benefited in a subtle but profound way. Westley argues that salvation is ultimately not individual but communal, as "shared prayer" and shared dialogue create an intimacy of love and faith between "spiritual companions."[26] As one group member plainly said, "To share the fruits of the Holy Spirit at work is natural."

In one of the younger groups, there was a very full and honest faith-sharing episode during the *lectio* one evening, the

---

26. Westley, *Good Things Happen*, 84.

scripture passage being very apt and experientially identifiable to those present. Through the willing responses by *each* member of the group, the shared experience was unmistakably strong. All commented on its felt effect. The female facilitator, a natural leader whose strength lay in being able to nourish others' participation in the group, had, by her encouragement and personal example, opened the way so that the Divine Therapist could work in each person in the dynamic emptying and healing process which Keating compares to uncovering past civilizations at the site of an archaeological tell.[27] Indeed, there is no more powerful incentive for individual perseverance than to hear someone else in the group in a non-critical atmosphere of mutual respect, echoing one's own sentiment, whether it be fear, doubt, guilt, or joy. One experience of such faith-sharing removes the perception of threat so that the individuals are increasingly willing to speak and to share with friends their successes and difficulties. Perhaps this intensifying of group identity happens with time anyway; but such an experience as the above accelerates it, molds it, clarifies it for all to see. A group, therefore, can age both in natural time and through intense experiences, just as a person can. One is reminded of the early non-hierarchical Christian community whose unity, intensified surely by its marginal status and by persecution, was also reinforced through the building of intimate personal relationships of faith and revelation. An interesting parallel exists in the Indian Vedantic tradition where individual meditation has for centuries been complemented by group dialogue or *satsang*—the sharing of questions and insights arising from direct experience.

C. S. Lewis, in *Mere Christianity*, compares the emergence of "group personality" to the interlocking Persons of the Trinity. He says of the development of a common "spirit": "The individual members, when they are together, do really develop particular ways of talking and behaving which they would not have if they were apart. It is as if a sort of communal personality came

---

27. Keating, *Intimacy With God*, 83.

into existence."[28] Despite the danger of stereotypic categorization, I will give impressions of three group personalities, unique because the confluence of individuals is unique. The personality of the facilitator, however, is a prominent factor especially as it affects the core members who attend regularly.

In the adolescent group, which I called the "heart" group, there was an overwhelming presence in the two facilitators and several other core members (all of whom were women) of a strong devotion to the practice and to each other. They were very solicitous of each other, especially if one of them was sick or in need. Although these women lived alone and valued companionship, as one woman gratefully reported, this compassionate attitude sprang from the heart and cannot be reduced to functional needs alone.

The young group, whose introductory workshop and first four months' meetings I attended, was gangly and awkward at first; however, the group took on a quiet, trusting, low-key ambience after six months together. From the moment of gathering in front of the church and then entering to set up for the prayer meeting, the mood was quiet and reverential. The facilitator was himself a patient, quiet, and unassuming man. It appears that a confluence of factors, including the solemn beauty of the sanctuary setting, the modest, quiet presence of the facilitator, and the depth of contemplative devotion shown by one woman in particular created this group personality of quiet reverence.

The last example is just the opposite. This group, a combination of a mature group of three and a young, newly formed group of six to eight was spirited, enthusiastic, and social. Before and after the meetings, the air sparkled with rapid exchanges of conversation, witty repartees, and laughter. This joyful animation was reinforced by the enthusiasm of the facilitator who joined in the frolicking. But in between, in the boundaries of worship and prayer, the atmosphere became hushed as by unanimous unspoken consent, the members entered a timeless zone. This respect

---

28. C. S. Lewis, *Mere Christianity* (New York: Touchstone Books, 1996), 152.

for the task at hand was true of all the groups. If it was tres-passed—and I observed this only once when a woman came in late to a group during a preliminary scripture reading—everyone felt it, like a tear in the skin. Instead of quietly sitting down, she began talking to the group; the glaring quality of the interruption was clear to all but her.

I would suggest that the jovial bantering and camaraderie displayed in this third example of group personality was not an extraneous or detracting factor but rather an integral part in the deepening of group practice in Centering Prayer and in group bonding *for those individuals.* Indeed, students of group process assert that group maturation depends upon the discernment and periodic reassessment of the appropriate balance between efforts given to *task* (Centering Prayer and attendant format) and *process,* or the building of interpersonal relationships.[29]

Another insight into the organic development of groups comes from anthropologist Victor Turner's study, *The Ritual Process.*[30] Enlarging on the sequence of tribal rites of passage, Turner describes a first stage of separation by the initiates, or any group that wishes to distinguish itself, from the ordinary consciousness of everyday life to share a heightened or *liminal* experience of a sacred, transformative nature in a special place. Instructed by the elders in the traditions and myths of the tribe—or analogously, in the case of CO, instructed in the Christian spiritual mystic tradition through a contemplative practice reworked by three Benedictine monks and furthered in the individual by the Holy Spirit—these "called" compatriots form an egalitarian, intimate bonding or *communitas* as they enter the purifying space of spiritual growth. This second stage is followed by reaggregation or a return of the group members to normal social life, but now bearing within their souls a finer sense of truth.

---

29. Shaffer and Anundsen, *Creating Community Anywhere,* 239.

30. Victor Turner, *The Ritual Process* (Ithaca, N.Y.: Cornell University Press, 1969).

Structure

THE STRUCTURE OF the Centering Prayer weekly group meeting is the house within which the group lives and grows. It consists of features of format and procedure which serve as walls and furniture for the house. Though fairly uniform in following Keating's format suggestions in *Open Mind, Open Heart,* each group displays slight variations in the floor plan design and are thus self-governing and creative in this sense.[31] Most groups begin with a prayer which varies from a selection from the Divine Office of the day to self-composed prayers. This introductory prayer is followed by the essential task or purpose of Centering Prayer which is divided into two *sits,* as some members refer to the two twenty-minute periods. A meditative walk divides these two periods of Centering Prayer. Usually a reciting of the Lord's Prayer follows, either slowly and quietly delivered by the facilitator as Keating suggests or recited by everyone. This latter choice often unwittingly triggers the habit of what could be called "assembly line" or rote praying. A period of *lectio divina,* or *collatio* (group *lectio*), follows, accompanied by varied degrees of group response or faith-sharing. In one group, a parish priest who practices Centering Prayer comes once a month to discuss with the group questions and experiences regarding the practice; this event substitutes for *lectio.* In another group, the meditative walk and one sit were eliminated. Reading from a spiritual book chosen by the facilitator substituted for *lectio*; sometimes a brief group response was elicited. This group was experiencing problems with stability when I first visited, but the devotion of the several core members gave constancy. One last variation in the group format is the content of final prayers, which may be self-composed but are usually from Catholic liturgy (e.g., "Glory be," "Hail Mary"). A thorn in some of the conversations at conferences and business meetings has been whether some Centering Prayer groups have over emphasized the Catholic element and in doing so have compromised the Christian and ecumenical vision of CO.

---

31. Keating, *Open Mind, Open Heart,* 135–36.

An effort to permit flexibility and thus avoid the historically hierarchical, top-down authoritarian Catholic structure is observable not only in the loosely-structured network of CO with its democratic, egalitarian Board of Trustees, faculty, staff, and its series of CO national conferences (whose aim is to reach decisions on CO policy and development by consensus), but also in the small group grassroots environment. I have described the variations which groups insert into the group meeting. There are other indications also. For example, I observed that most facilitators back off from words like *instruction, rules,* or *standardization,* preferring words such as *suggestion* or *invitation* which signal a respect for one's peers, lay or religious, and a valuation of the American ritual of individual choice. At a recent day intensive the presiding leader said:

> We're passing out evaluation forms later; it's important what people feel about the day's experience. CO is not a leadership thing, not Thomas or anyone dictating what we should do. It's grassroots.

Sometimes the non-coercive approach carries with it some ambiguity. As one facilitator said to me:

> I don't like to appear to tell people what to do. If they're late, for example, it's disruptive but I feel awkward saying anything. One person had a psychological problem we couldn't deal with . . . we got help though.

There is a genuine humility in the desire to allow people room to discover for themselves their commitment to the practice and to the group, to "let them be led by the Holy Spirit." Since Vatican II, a perspective has spread which acknowledges the dignity of all Christians as the mystical Body of Christ. However, the reminder from Keating that in true Christian doctrine the human essence is defined not as sin, which is the imposition of the false-self, but as the indwelling Holy Spirit still surprises and stimulates practitioners, particularly Catholics. As one person remarked, putting her hand to her heart, "I'm still getting used to realizing that the Holy Spirit is here, in me, the divine as my real self."

As an earlier example showed, the inclusion of faith-sharing in the format of the group meeting was observed to greatly assist both the individual—through the healing and revealing power of speaking the truth and being listened to without criticism—and the group — through the tightening of the spiritual/social bonds between people.

Another variation besides that of format is the alternating of facilitators. Two groups were experimenting with this rotation while I was a visitor. In one group, the rotation was working because the small group of four had been together for five years, and each member was well versed in procedure. The initial facilitator and still acting head of the group said that he believed "empowerment" was necessary. In the second group, which was much younger and more populous, there was also a desire to share responsibility. However, as the two initial facilitators discovered, rotating—especially in a weekly fashion of volunteers—sometimes engaged neophytes who were either not comfortable with or knowledgeable about the suggested format.

There are minor roles of leadership which are designated to other members by the facilitator—that of timer, for instance. For the most part, facilitators are very aware of their leadership role and wish to minimize its impact by gestures of humility. The permission inherent in CO for experimentation, as CO itself is a structural experiment, are signs I believe of a desire for inclusion, equality, and creativity in an egalitarian atmosphere. This non-authoritarian philosophy is not only imperative for community-building but congenial to the American mind-set.[32]

Setting

AS A PART of structure, the setting of an evening gathering played an interesting contextual role. [33] Setting can facilitate the experience of the *holy* and, in this way, elevate and set apart, as Durkheim, Otto, and others have argued, the *sacred* from the *profane*.[34] In a larger

---

32. Peck in *The Different Drum*, 93 stresses the incompatibility of true community and autocratic structure.

33. All seven groups which I visited met on a weekday evening. Six of the groups met from 6:30–8 P.M. One group met from 7:30–9 P.M.

34. See Emile Durkheim, *The Elementary Forms of Religious Life* (New York: The Free Press, 1965) and Rudolf Otto, *The Idea of the Holy* (London: Oxford University Press, 1950).

context, however, this concept of separation is flawed, as Keating maintains, since the fruits of Centering Prayer appear in ordinary life, elevating that life and thus integrating what has been mistakenly reduced to an inferior position of the *worldly* with the *otherworldly*.[35] One enters Otto's *mysterium* of the *holy* or *numinous* realm through entering the sphere of everyday activity with heightened attention and love. Such an attitude is exemplified, for example, in St. Terese of Lisieux's "picking up a pin for God," the Zen practice of mindfulness, and Simone Weil's pithy challenge that full attention to life's activities is prayer.[36]

Nevertheless, the function of setting in the weekly meeting is to remind participants of the special purpose for which they are gathered and thus distinguish worldly and otherworldy realms in order to ultimately integrate them. First, each group had to accept the setting as a given: it was a space allotted to the group by the parish which housed it, the quality of which varied from place to place. What became interesting to me as an observer were the responses of the group members to the given.[37] Secondly, the setting as place consists of an outer room of neighborly socializing and an inner room of practice which corresponds to the sanctuary of the heart where silence and reverence pervade, where with one's eyes closed, mind and heart receptive and willing, the practitioner as no-person is conducted into a personal relationship with God.

The differentiation between these two rooms is set by the group, apparently unconsciously, or perhaps out of a common

---

35. CO Formation Training Manual; Lecture #4, 17–19.

36. Simone Weil, *Gravity and Grace* (London: Routledge and Kegan Paul, 1952), 105–6.

37. The "given" also includes the fact that groups met in churches only, not in houses. At conferences, I have spoken with people whose groups did meet in one of the members' houses. In one case, it was a "closed" group. One facilitator in New York City explained that some newcomers to Centering Prayer groups might feel excluded or uncomfortable meeting in someone's home; this remark echoes the modern concept of "home" as an inviolable private sphere. It also affirms a refreshing post–Vatican II definition of church as an inclusive, non-restrictive meeting place.

sense of purpose. Sometimes the rooms were geographically sep-
arated. At one parish, for example, the group promptly congre-
gated in the front lobby, greeted each other warmly and chatted
until five minutes before the meeting began. The facilitator had
prepared the room earlier. At 7:25 everyone moved through the
door, down the corridor, and into a small anteroom adjacent to
the sanctuary which had formerly been a confessional. A stained
glass window, two statues of saints, and rich mahogany wood pan-
eling invited the prayerful into a solemn atmosphere in which all
conversation ceased. The format proceeded in this conducive
atmosphere enhanced by the creative use of taped music—a
soothing flute melody in repeated doses—which divided the
prayer sessions as a substitute for the usual timer gadget. This
group concluded its meeting with voluntary prayer offerings for
other people. Although whispered conversation began as people
got up, put on their coats, and left the inner room, it wasn't until
the corridor and lobby were reached that the demeanor of reverence was shed for more boisterous socializing. When I asked
members about their place of worship, they spoke appreciatively
of "this special setting" as well as of the young parish priest who
joined them once a month. The changes in setting from the beginning to the end of the evening symbolically demonstrate the
changes in psychological states described in Turner's *ritual process*.

   The setting of another group demonstrates in stark contrast
the necessity for the group sometimes to *create* a prayerful atmosphere; as Westley puts it, "our spiritual experiences consecrate
the places where they occur."[38] The given in this case was a small
utility room in the rectory in which the commercial carpeting,
undecorated white walls, florescent lights, and gray metal folding
chairs suited a business meeting rather than a prayer meeting.
The group, however, took it upon itself to create an inner room
of shared solitude and beauty. As the members arrived, they
fetched a small table from the lobby, covered it with a tapestry
cloth and put a large white candle on it as centerpiece. Using this
adorned table as the ritual center of the small room, the group set

---

38. Westley, *Good Things Happen*, 108.

chairs around it. People sat down to talk and share the day's events until the facilitator or another member lit the candle. All talk hushed as someone turned off the bare florescent light with its mindless hum. Around the magical candlelight, members listened to scripture by flashlight, centered, walked, centered, and participated in *lectio divina*. A bland, even detracting setting had been transformed into a place of ritual celebration.

Two last examples of setting are revealing. In both, the church sanctuary was made available. Its ambience had the power to conduct a practitioner into the silence and veneration of decades of worshipers; this heritage the members acknowledged in gratitude. One group had the joy of seeing their priest, as peer, join them periodically. In the other church, the group was often moved from one room to another because the parish was very active. Sometimes the place was the sanctuary. I remember experiencing the awe of procession-like walks down aisles bordered by myriad, flickering votive candles lighting the dark vaulted space. On one occasion, however, a vibrant Spanish mission service occupied the sanctuary. Down to two participants that night, the facilitator and I were given a small nondescript room below the sanctuary. To my right, sounds of guitar, tambourines, and enthusiastic singing shot through the wall; to my left, an exercise class was vigorously in progress. It was a memorable occasion. I remembered Keating's example of street sounds attracting the attention away from the important conversation between the soul and God. We persevered, and afterwards enjoyed a stimulating conversation about the virtues of adaptability, a sense of humor, and the importance of remembering that the true inner room is the attentive, loving heart.

Setting as place, therefore, is a variable which can influence the life of the group, as can the presence of an enthusiastic priest and/or a supportive parish. The particular contextual design of these elements was different in each of the seven groups. However, environment is also self-created (or rather group-created), reflecting the intention and commitment to practice of each individual in a mood of group solidarity: these are the "keys to the kingdom."

Volunteerism and Commitment

THE AMERICAN DEMOCRATIC tradition is a natural environment for CO as a loosely-structured, grassroots spiritual network within the Church to sprout and grow. Its representative governing bodies of lay and religious volunteers and its innovative restoration of contemplative practice for the individual fits a cultural tradition which supports individual and group creativity in both religious and secular realms. Jon Butler, in *Awash in a Sea of Faith*, enumerates the plethora of eighteenth and nineteenth century religious denominations and revivalist spiritual movements which celebrated egalitarianism, experimentation, experiential spirituality, and pluralism. This rich tradition flows into the twentieth century. Furthermore, the democratic image has valued flexibility and tolerance over coercion. Even exceptions such as the doctrinaire Puritan ethic in New England, while partaking of the cultural mandate of religious liberty, prefigured its own demise by a rigid authoritarian philosophy. In like manner, modern day fundamentalist orthodoxy, though vocal in religious and political spheres, is overshadowed by a cultural inclination to more moderate norms of action. The concept of leadership in CO follows St. Paul's analogy of the body with its organs functioning to benefit the whole organism (Rom. 12). From the charisma of Father Keating to the varied gifts of group members, natural leaders arise, exuding authority in word and action; but it is my observation that the remembrance of the source of true authority—the Holy Spirit—often inserts itself, restraining claims of the prideful false self.

It can be argued that the Roman Catholic Church in America has absorbed the nation's democratic cultural traits. From the 1830s onward, certain bishops led a movement to "unite church with the age."[39] John Carroll, for example, argued for a vernacular liturgy, a cooperation with Protestants, and the right of the American Church to choose its own bishops. Isaac Hecker, a Paulist Father in the 1880s, preached and wrote about the

---

39. Jay P. Dolan, *The American Catholic Experience* (Notre Dame, Ind.: University of Notre Dame Press, 1992), 309.

indwelling Spirit as the primary focus of the Catholic faith, that therefore it is the Church's fundamental duty to nourish the spiritual development of the laity.[40] Bishop John Ireland and Bronson Alcott of the Transcendentalist movement concurred: the mystical dimension is the Church's main task and the work of each individual. Although these voices in the wilderness were criticized by the Vatican at the time, their prophetic message prefigured Vatican II.

Stirred by lay reform movements in Europe and America in the 1950s, the Church in the 1960s erupted along with other social and political upheavals of the era as Vatican II "turned Catholicism on its head."[41] The symbolic removal of the tiara by John XXIII as he entered the Vatican Council presaged a changing image of Church from static institutional top-down teaching authority to Church as *People of God* and *Mystical Body* of peers. Vatican II injunctions to rediscover Christian spiritual roots of contemplative practice and community, while reaching out simultaneously to accommodate modern needs and to dialogue with other religions, inspired a democratic surge of creative experiments of which CO is an example.

The American democratic tradition gives the individual freedom to join whatever church or other voluntary association he or she wishes; but with that action comes a responsibility to that collective voice. This commitment was called by men and women of Ben Franklin's time *civic duty*. As mentioned earlier, certain observers of modern American society see a cultural withdrawal from this act of commitment, a burrowing into the self-absorption of a therapeutic culture centered on "me."[42] What may begin as a genuine search for self-identity deteriorates into narcissism, exacerbated by a modern era obsessed with material consumerism and impersonal global technologies, and plagued by massive ecological and nuclear risks.[43]

---

40. Ibid., 307.
41. Ibid., 426.
42. Bellah et al., *Habits of the Heart*, chap. 5.
43. See Anthony Giddens, *The Consequences of Modernity* (Stanford: Stanford University Press, 1990) and Lasch, *The Culture of Narcissism*.

How, if at all, do these modern currents in American and global culture resonate in CO as it is situated in American and Catholic history? A comment I heard a number of times while participating in CO activities claimed that, "because CO is voluntary we can't force anyone to attend or expect too much from them in the way of service; it's their free choice."[44] This statement acknowledges the respect and liberty due the individual inherent in American custom. It may also be a sentiment which counteracts in a positive, compassionate manner the historical insistence of the hierarchical Church on strict obedience to rules emanating from a sanctified church tradition. Rather, CO's philosophy calls upon an equally legitimate origin of action: the work of the indwelling Holy Spirit in the individual "whose call to commitment may or may not be heard."[45] One evening, as a group of us walked across town after the Centering Prayer meeting, a woman spoke of her appreciation for this lack of coercion. Her words were followed by echoing agreement from the other members:

> Group members come and go, as it should be. I reserve this evening because I want to, as a commitment. It needs to be loose, like Mass is now. You go because you want to, not because you're feeling guilty and you'll go to Hell. That's not true anymore—I hope.

Because the small group is the backbone of CO, it may be important to consider whether and how much such slang Americanisms as *do your own thing* or *go for it* (implying *by yourself*) in expressing a cultural allegiance to "what I want when I want it" insidiously infect voluntary associations, including CO, interfering with group stability and growth. If spiritual individuation depends on strong group support, then the issue of volunteerism and commitment may need to be more assiduously addressed. With the burgeoning of American affluence has arisen a cultural misconception about volunteerism which relegates it to an inferior position, way below the icon of making a living—rather like a disposable item or an

---

44. Paraphrased from group member remarks.
45. Ibid.

afterthought. This psychology needs adjustment. Because volunteers are engaged in an activity with no material pay, it is obviously the psychological, spiritual, and communal benefits which are sought. In fact, this voluntary involvement in many cases means more to a person than his or her job. Volunteers *want* to be there, *are* committed to some degree, and *will* give of their time if asked. CO can legitimately take advantage of this fact in respectful encouragement of regular attendance at group meetings as well as training weekends for facilitators and interested group members, such as those presently being offered in Los Angeles.

"Where two or three are gathered": The Power of the Small Group Process

IN THIS LAST section, I wish to offer an assessment of the strengths of CO and suggestions for its further growth based upon my experience with the Manhattan groups. A major strength of CO is its fulfillment, through the promotion of Centering Prayer, of the need in the Church and in American society for a retrieval and exploration of the mystic dimension of religious life.[46] Cultivating "intimacy with God," as Keating calls it, is the quintessential human activity which can satisfy psychological and spiritual hunger in an era when the preoccupation with therapies to massage and fix the ego or false self promise questionable antidotes for individual and social malaise.

The current malaise can be viewed as a consequence of a process of fragmentation that has progressively alienated human beings from their fellows, from technology, from nature, from the world they have constructed, and most of all from himself. This alienation, diagnosed as schizophrenia by psychologist Laing and Bateson, an anthropologist, can be traced to the euphoria of the seventeenth- and eighteenth-century Enlightenment when human reason, in its creative manipulation

---

46. For more on these themes see Bellah et al., *Habits of the Heart* and Cousins, *Christ in the Twenty-First Century*.

of nature, decided it could dispense with God.[47] The dire results of the Cartesian split of mind from body and earth from spirit are still experienced today.[48] Centering prayer, through the agency of CO, offers a means to heal this fragmentation by integrating presumed dualities perceived as opposed: in particular, male/female, contemplation/action, me/God, Christianity/other religions, and individual/community. These integrations are accomplished through the remembrance of a third mediating and unifying force. C. S. Lewis describes the process eloquently in *Mere Christianity*: "the devil . . . always sends errors into the world as pairs—pairs of opposites. . . . We have to . . . go straight through between both errors."[49]

The first pair—male/female—is released from a polar antagonism by recognition of a human nature which subsumes, without eradicating, gender differences. In contemplative practices such as Centering Prayer, the non-rational faculties usually associated with the feminine principle dominate over rational faculties. Mystic literature abounds with examples of the necessary of drawing out of the hidden "feminine" gifts of intuition, receptivity, and passionate surrender of the heart. The second set of presumed opposites—contemplation and action—are recognized as complementary in Centering Prayer. The fruits of practice, such as detachment, non-judgment, and compassion, are seen as the natural translation of contemplation into action.

An interesting paradox obtains in resolving the me-God dichotomy. First, one must ask who is this "me?" As Keating and Merton before him insist, understanding the difference between the true self and the false self is crucial. A personal relationship with God is a relationship through the indwelling Holy Spirit

---

47. See R. D. Laing, *The Divided Self* (London: Penguin Books, 1990); Gregory Bateson, *Steps to an Ecology of Mind* (San Francisco: Chandler Publishing Co., 1972).

48. See Louis Dupre, *Passage to Modernity* (New Haven: Yale University Press, 1993) and Hannah Arendt, *The Human Condition* (Chicago: University of Chicago Press, 1958) on the shift from medieval-spiritual to modern-materialist paradigms.

49. Lewis, *Mere Christianity*, 161.

which defuses and transforms the false self as it releases from bondage the true self or that which is divine—the real person. Moreover, the inclusivity and ecumenism of CO mean that it can embrace other religions without diluting the integrity of those religions or compromising its own Christian beliefs; rather, as the late Cardinal Bernardin envisioned, it is a matter of finding a "common ground."

Lastly, an integration of the needs of individual and community is possible through the CO network of small groups which provide a communal environment in which individual practice is enhanced. These small groups offer the individual the spiritual incentive of other like-minded travelers and furnish a protective shield against the temptations and distractions of an economically fixated American and global society. It may be that, just as political repression and poverty have inspired the creation of base ecclesial communities in Latin America, so, at the other pole, affluence and greed in America have elicited an urgency to build communities visible in the rise of the communitarian movement and the increase of multifaceted support groups.

The communitarian philosophy proposes an inherent reciprocity between individual and group: "The *I* and *We* are in perpetual creative conflict . . . the individual's aims are important, but they are framed within the traditions and needs of the group."[50] Corresponding to Peck's final group phase of *community*, Shaffer and Anundsen propose the establishment of *synergy*, a condition of flow in which individual and group are so in tune that each feeds the other simultaneously.[51] The centering group, which experienced a momentary heightening of spiritual and social consciousness one evening through prayer and faith-sharing, had a taste of this impulse of synergy.

CO's several covenanted communities as well as the weekly small groups dotted across the country and globe attest to CO's contribution to this upstream swim against the current of a

---

50. Harry C. Triandis, *Individualism and Collectivism* (Boulder, Colo.: Westview Press, 1995), 38–39.

51. Shaffer and Anundsen, *Creating Community Anywhere*, 209–16.

cultural bias which has progressively devalued group solidarity while elevating individual ambition. However, nurturing the dynamic tension between the individual and group requires continuous vigilance and work. Ewert Cousins, a noted Christian theologian, seems to think that the tide is necessarily turning. In a recent interview in *The Christian Century,* he argues that

> Spirituality in all of the major religions of the world—for example, in Christianity, Hinduism and Buddhism—has been very individualistic. It is true that these religions have nurtured social concerns and have also been involved with issues relating to the larger community. Nevertheless, their chief focus has been largely focused upon the individual. In the recent past [within the last ten years] a shift has been under way however [towards a community focus].[52]

David Morgan, a pioneer in ecumenical community living based on Centering Prayer practice, speaks of the significance of this kind of primary group in the modern era:

> The loss of family ties and common goals that formerly fused people together has left a vacuum that only commitment to relationship rather than strategy can heal . . . only a prayerful, listening community can effect true healing from brokenness and the promised rest of divine union.[53]

CO can be a forerunner in fostering a cultural understanding of the link between commitment to a group's development and the individual's own spiritual growth by educating group members in the dynamics of group process. Thus the groups themselves will choose full commitment in the concrete form, for example, of regular attendance. An organism grows by its own laws, but it is important to be *aware* of those laws so as to creatively assist in their unfolding. For example, according to Shaffer and Anundsen, phase one involves the establishment of the group. This phase requires a tighter hold by the facilitator or

---

52. Leo D. Lefebure, "Beyond Scapegoating: a Conversation with Rene Girard and Ewert Cousins," *The Christian Century* 115:11 (1998): 372–75.

53. David Morgan, "Christian Community and Centering Prayer," *Centering Prayer in Daily Life and Ministry,* ed. Gustave Reininger (New York: Continuum, 1998), 102.

leader than the later stages when authority is delegated and the empowerment of all group members as "leaders" in different capacities can occur.[54] It follows that in a CO group, rotation of facilitators, if desired by the group, should await this maturing process. This waiting did not occur in the adolescent group described earlier because of the good intention to include everyone by sharing power; this decision was reversed, however, when it became obvious that some members did not yet have sufficient experience in centering and in the group format to facilitate.

Another law of group theory which directly affects CO small groups is the gradual attainment through synergy of what Shaffer and Anundsen call *silent attunement*.[55] Peck identifies this silence as the "ultimate facilitator of emptiness" which is the necessary letting-go bridge to community.[56] It is Westley's "law of weakness" and Keating's *unloading* and *evacuation* of the constrictive notions and repressed feelings of the false self system.[57] Although this ease in the silence of one another's presence was observed in the mature groups, it is my observation that any aged group can move to a habitual experience of this silent attunement that naturally ensues from receptivity to the silence of the Holy Spirit, so long as a conscious awareness and practice of silence within the enclosure of prayer activities is encouraged by the facilitator and group members.

The several parts of the format invite the appreciation of silence. The intellectual stimulation of *lectio*, for example, engages mind and heart; and Centering Prayer itself rests in silence. But it is also the unhurried transitions between parts of the format, the slow recitation—as advised by Keating—of the Lord's Prayer, and—when it is encouraged—the self-disclosure of faith-sharing surrounded by silent appreciation, that stretch out the silent space in which the individual can grow and the group bond. As the atmosphere of loving, positive reinforcement

----

54. Shaffer and Anundsen, *Creating Community Anywhere*, 276.
55. Ibid., 256.
56. Peck, *The Different Drum*, 130.
57. Westley, *Good Things Happen*, 110; Keating, *Intimacy With God*, 75–84.

and trust deepens, the practitioner has a chance to experience an alternate mode of existence in which the fast pace and mechanical nature of ordinary living is glaringly juxtaposed to this supportive, receptive, and relaxed environment. As one group member who had been practicing with a Tuesday group for only three months said:

> I'm not used to silence with God, to listening. Maybe He'll tell me to do something I don't want to! But when I go home on Tuesdays I'm so happy to just be quiet; no TV or phone calls. I tell my friends to call me Monday night. I'm becoming aware of a nonproductive pace of life in the city; there's no quiet.

It may be that the very factors of New York City life that promote isolation, individualist aggression, excessive noise (outside and inside the head!), and a frenzied pace of living mandate a strong compensatory measure in the collective, unhurried, enriching, quiet experience of friendship founded on spiritual practice within a small group. Furthermore, interaction *between* such groups through frequent day intensives or joint projects could further strengthen the network horizontally at the same time that lines of communication in the vertical direction are tightened. It is an administrative art to combine the flexibility and freedom of action which characterize a loosely-structured network with the organizational cohesion necessary to offset group isolation.

In my opinion, it is in the nurturing of group self-awareness bound to the transformative spiritual practice of Centering Prayer that CO can minister to the needs of the twenty-first century. Let me give an example: a young woman who had just come over from Hungary joined one of the Centering Prayer groups I was visiting. She said she still corresponded with the close-knit Bible study group in her homeland, and that she was glad to find a meaningful prayer experience in this country. She wrote on her response form the following:

> The imperative is that a community be formed. This is done by creating a loving environment, and that is done by fostering trust and tolerance. The goal of my existence is tied up with others. It is the [spiritual] connection with others that strengthens me.

Her insistence on collective practice reflected an historical image of America as an immigrant nation, tied together by networks of national origin as it simultaneously attempted to find a new unity. We now enter a new millennium in a different, global context, but the need for community based on spirituality is still imperative, perhaps more so. Christ, the model of transformation for Christians, said, according to the John 13:34, "A new commandment I give unto you. That ye love one another as I have loved you." This is community.

Keating, reflecting on the shift in perspective in which CO, a form of community, emerged to enfold individuals into a common purpose said that

> It was not with a view to forming a community that we started it [Centering Prayer] . . . my conviction grew that we could not introduce the contemplative life or people without some kind of ongoing formation or support system. Actually that was the original purpose of primitive monastic life whether it was conscious or not. . . . One of the great supports of migration, I suppose, is flying in flocks. A dangerous and long journey to nowhere needs company.[58]

Jesus' words, "For where two or three are gathered in My name there am I in their midst," is not just a nice sentiment. It works. In today's precarious world, it is imperative that we practice it.

---

58. Thomas Keating, June 6, 1993, personal statement on Contemplative Outreach Vision, 1–2.

8 ※

Introducing Centering Prayer into the Curriculum at an Ecumenical Seminary: A Call to Personal and Systemic Conversion

GEORGE F. CAIRNS

Reluctantly Lured Back into the Church

I ENTERED SEMINARY as a student in 1987 seeking a vocation, although I didn't know it at the time. Trained both as an experimental psychologist doing research in early infant development for about eight years and then as a clinical psychologist who had worked with marginalized people for about ten years, I was seeking ways of healing that run deeper than the ways I had employed in the past. My training in psychology and my work as a community activist during the civil rights, antiwar, and feminist movements of the 1960s and 1970s had left me alienated from the church. Like many people of my generation, I saw the organized church as ethically bankrupt, spiritually anemic, and inauthentic.

During many of these years away from the church, I continued to seek for deeper meaning than the self-actualization
that contemporary psychology had to offer and beyond the self-
righteousness and short-term achievements that frenzied social
action produced. At the same time, I continued to search for
deeper meaning in life. Like many others, I looked East and
began a regular sitting practice in the Zen tradition, ultimately
having some contact with Danen Katagiri Roshi, a Zen master in
the Soto Zen tradition. During this period, I was also deeply
drawn to solitude in the wilderness. As this path deepened, I
spent a week in solitude on an island sacred to native people and
received a grace-filled vision that undermined my usual materi-
alist worldview.

The Seminary Context

So HERE I came, entering seminary with a largely Buddhist prayer
life and visions gifted by God through the openings provided in
solitude in nature. I first entered a seminary affiliated with the
University of Chicago Divinity School. During an initial interview when I was encouraged to apply for an M.Div./Ph.D. program, I mentioned to the theologian with whom I was conversing that I regarded myself as a mystic given the powerful visions
that I had experienced. He dryly replied, "We don't have many
mystics around here." As I was later to find out, this was something of an understatement.

During the first year at this seminary, the flatness and arid-
ity of the formal and informal curriculum discouraged me.
There seemed to be only one kind of acceptable way of speaking: rational, empirical argumentation. One friend later said to
me that the rules for success at the University of Chicago (and
by extension the surrounding seminaries) were "Read everything, remember it all, and be really smart." During the course
of my first year, students were asked to write reflection papers
regarding the curriculum at the seminary as part of preparation
for an upcoming accreditation visit. By this time, I was so dis-
illusioned that I began my paper with a quote by William Blake

that summed up my overall response to seminary education at this time.[1]

> Now I a fourfold vision see,
> And a fourfold vision is given to me;
> 'Tis fourfold in my supreme delight
> And threefold in soft Beulah's night
> And twofold always. May God us keep
> From Single vision & Newton's sleep.
>
> —William Blake
> November 22, 1802[2]

Shortly after this time, I moved to the Chicago Theological Seminary (CTS) where I continued my studies. I was drawn to this seminary for a variety of reasons: its ecumenicity (there are people from the Jewish, Catholic, and Protestant traditions studying in the five degree programs); its theological and engaged commitment to issues of justice; its excellence with its multiracial and multicultural faculty and students; its long history of engaging the social sciences with theological reflection; and its commitment to theological education as a constructive process that includes experience as one valued source for theological reflection.

CTS, while affiliated with the United Church of Christ, accepts students from all Protestant denominations into its M.Div. program. This policy results in an extremely broad range of theological orientations with correspondingly diverse communities of accountability that ultimately make decisions about each student's call to ministry and appropriateness for ordination. It is a continuing struggle to seek common ground while honoring all students' particular journeys in ministry and their ecclesial communities.

The seminary does this in a variety of ways. The first is to require all M.Div. students to develop their unique theological position (partially influenced by the credo of "Read everything, remember it all, and be really smart."). The second is to offer common worship,

---

1. I would like to view this response as simple truth-telling about the "single vision" of the seminary curriculum, but, as I continue the process of prayer, I understand that all of my motivations are mixed and that this response, while accurate, also had elements of my grandiosity, self-importance, and anger.

2. Robert Bly, ed., *News of the Universe: Poems of Twofold Consciousness* (San Francisco: Sierra Club Books, 1980), 29.

followed by a shared meal led by virtually all sectors of the community. I believe that the third (and most recently introduced) way is to offer a common contemplative practice that excludes no one from the process. The method that has deeply influenced me and that I have helped introduce into the seminary is Centering Prayer.

Shortly after arriving at seminary, some Catholic friends who were passing through town and knew that my wife Nancy and I continued a meditation practice in the Zen tradition introduced us to Centering Prayer, which they had just discovered as well as an early version of Fr. Thomas's *Open Mind, Open Heart.* Delighted to have found a compelling practice within the Christian tradition, I immediately shifted to practicing Centering Prayer on a regular basis. This process has changed my life. While in seminary, I continued the path of service, developing a street ministry and encouraging small faith communities in flop houses. The ministry was supported increasingly from sources deeper than my intentional plans.[3] Let me say here that contemplative prayer has been a part of my developing call to ministry and has under girded this ministry of service from the very beginning. I understood this in some ways then and continue to discover other ways in which prayer has deepened this work.

The first course I took was on mysticism. As a survey course it examined a few contemporary writers and several earlier spiritual theologians. An extremely talented professor who had a deep grounding in the human potential movements of the 1960s and 1970s taught it. I believe that he, like me, was attempting to extend the understanding of who God means us to be that goes beyond the self-actualization and peak experiences described by such theorists as Maslow.[4] My sense is that our collective understandings were still

---

3. I have written elsewhere about this process of contemplation and action. See George Cairns, "Socially Engaged Christianity: One Example of Contemplation and Action," in Wayne Teasdale and George Cairns, eds., *The Community of Religions: Voices and Images of the Parliament of the World's Religions* (New York: Continuum, 1996), 121–24.

4. Please see the following for more information regarding this worldview: Abraham Maslow, *Religions, Values and Peak Experiences* (New York: Penguin Books, 1976); Abraham Maslow, *The Farther Reaches of Human Experience* (New York: Penguin Books, 1976).

primarily based in the social sciences. I know that for myself, though I had read *Open Mind, Open Heart* many times and taught using it, it was only when I began the series of retreats offered by Contemplative Outreach (CO) that I began to understand the profound and more radical nature of the process both experientially and theologically.

Practical Theology of Mysticism

DURING MY LAST year as a student in the M.Div. program at the seminary, I volunteered to teach a course titled "Practical Theology of Mysticism (PTM)." I intentionally chose this provocative title to challenge the prevailing world view in the seminary communities that contemplation was totally otherworldly and impractical. This view was nicely summed up by my wife Nancy who, rightly suspicious of seminary technobabble, said, "The title of this course is a triple oxymoron!"

I believe that there were several novel aspects of this course that have all been included in succeeding courses on Centering Prayer. First, a reading list included extensive material from the field of transpersonal psychology, which went beyond the humanistic psychologies that birthed it and began to study issues of spirituality directly. Although still maintaining a primarily empirical and materialistic bias, some writers in the field demonstrated increased openings to the transcendent. Other readings included such anti-spiritual writings as the Group for the Advancement of Psychiatry's report,[5] which largely pathologized profound religious experience, and the results of Greeley and McCready, which indicated how often people had such experiences and how unlikely they were to seek out clergy for advice regarding them.[6] *Open Mind, Open Heart* was also a required text.

---

5. Group for the Advancement of Psychiatry, "What Mysticism Is," reprinted in Daniel Colemen and Richard Davidson eds. *Consciousness: The Brain, States of Awareness, and Alternate Realities.* (New York: Irvington Publishers), 187–90.

6. Andrew Greeley and William McCready, "Are We a Nation of Mystics?" reprinted in Daniel Colemen and Richard Davidson, eds., *Consciousness: The Brain, States of Awareness, and Alternate Realities* (New York: Irvington Publishers), 178–83.

A second innovative requirement was that all participants engage in a twenty-minute period of Centering Prayer on a daily basis for the duration of the course. While there was some initial grousing about, "Why do we all have to do the same thing?" almost everyone, from the start, found ways to accommodate Centering Prayer into their daily prayer life. I pressed this issue from the start, indicating that we, as a community of support and accountability, needed a common praxis for our interior work. As an elective, this course was required of no one; and to my knowledge, no one dropped the course or any that followed because of this requirement.

A third novel aspect of this course and all that followed is that each three-hour class began with a twenty-minute period of Centering Prayer. I had several reasons for doing this. First, I believe that this period of prayer, when we intentionally consent to God's movement in our lives, provided openings to the Spirit that created the atmosphere for the rest of each class period and beyond. Second, it provided the common experience of shared Centering Prayer that would have been difficult otherwise. Third, the thought of spending twenty minutes of silence in an academic class is, to say the least, not a frequent practice in contemporary seminary education. I wished to communicate to my students, my colleagues, and to myself that this way of being together in silence was of value in the academic context. It was not some activity that should be divorced from the integrative process of understanding more about prayer.

Luckily, our seminary has a long history of praxis-based education where academic energies are distributed between actions in ministry and theological reflection on these actions while engaged with critical texts. I began to use terms like "internal praxis" to help all of us better understand the analogs that exist between the inner and outer work in our tradition. Both internal and external praxis involve some action; in this case, consenting to God's movement in our lives during periods of Centering Prayer is the action. Reflection is comparing the interior movements of the Spirit and its impact on our lives with one another and then conversing with the previous witnesses to the inner life—Scripture and the spiritual theologians in the tradition.

A fourth unusual aspect of these courses is that the course/instructor/student evaluation is unusual. These courses are always graded Pass/Fail. My wish is to open a wide range of exploration for the students as they engage the practice of Centering Prayer and encounter the cloud of witnesses who have come before us. It also seems a little presumptuous of me to grade someone's prayer life. For academic purposes, my covenant with the students is to write letters of recommendation based on the details of our work together rather than focusing on a letter grade as the focal point of our work. In-class written and verbal evaluations were also conducted. Individual written evaluations were completed anonymously and were returned directly to the academic dean's office. Group verbal feedback was elicited several times during the course with special emphasis on feedback at the end of the course.

One-on-one evaluation also took place when I met with each student, individually, for an hour at the end of the course. There were several reasons for this interview. First, I wished to discuss the student's reflection papers and integrative journal with him or her. Second, I wished to assist the student to continue his or her journey by helping him or her connect with additional resources such as ongoing Centering Prayer groups, spiritual directors, and with Contemplative Outreach. A lengthy annotated bibliography of works that I found helpful in my journey was often one focus of this conversation, as students resonated with particular strands of our tradition. Third, I wished to have a chance for an interactive evaluation of how helpful the course had been for the students.

"Practical Theology of Mysticism" was offered twice when I returned to the seminary as a faculty member after working for a time as a parish minister. During these offerings, the content of the course increasingly included texts on spiritual theology and less emphasis on transpersonal psychology. On reflection, I believe that this shift reflected my increased understanding of the Christian spiritual theological tradition and also reflected the existential shift in my life from primarily a secular psychologist to that of a minister and spiritual guide.

Crucial to this shift has been my increased involvement with CO. I now realize that it was only as I went through the sequence of training workshops CO offers that I began to understand fully—experientially and intellectually—the theological underpinnings for Centering Prayer. I am almost ashamed to admit that after regularly practicing Centering Prayer for over eight years and teaching it for three, I still had profound misunderstandings regarding subtle theological dimensions of the practice. What emerged from these understandings was an expanded and, I hope, more adequate introduction to contemplative prayer. Let's turn now to the new course that was the result.

Prayer as the Heart of Religious Leadership: Opening the Heart through Centering Prayer

ONE PROFOUND DIFFICULTY I encountered in the earlier courses was the lack of time to encourage the Centering Prayer practice, provide adequate time for reflection on the practice, provide the theological grounding for it, provide the larger context of spiritual theology, engage the social sciences, and provide insights for extending this experience into ministry. I proposed, through the Life-long Learning program at CTS to offer a two-quarter course that I hoped would eliminate these limitations. For the past two years, this expanded course, "Prayer as the Heart of Religious Leadership: Opening the Heart Through Centering Prayer," has been taught in winter/spring quarters to oversubscribed classes. This year it becomes part of the regular curriculum.

While it is largely based on the previous courses, there are several additions. First, I offered an introductory workshop to Centering Prayer during the first two class periods. Second, we expanded examination of Fr. Thomas's "Spiritual Journey" tapes and added additional readings in spiritual theology and prayer and leadership.[7] Third, we encouraged more small group work and added an optional silent retreat.

---

7. Please see the end of the chapter for a list of books required for the upcoming 1999 course.

The pattern of each three-hour class period following the introduction to Centering Prayer has remained largely the same after the first two classes: a period of twenty minutes of Centering Prayer, group reflection on our practice, reflection on the readings and the "Spiritual Journey" tape viewed the previous week, time in small groups, and then viewing the "Spiritual Journey" tape for the current week.

Some thoughts about the small groups: The first year I taught the course, thirty people signed up for it. While I limited enrollment to twenty the second year, there were still too many of us to allow for enough exploration of individual issues. Some students felt uncomfortable sharing with such a large group. The second year, I established more formal structure to small group work. I encouraged each small group of four to six people to covenant together for the duration of the course during their initial meeting. I asked that the covenant be written, that all participants sign it, and that copies be distributed to one another and to me. Given the diversity of the students, the only guidelines for the covenant were that people act together as a community of support and accountability and that they develop mutually agreed upon norms for their group. I agreed to act as a consultant to the small groups as needed, which, as it turned out, was seldom. Many students found the intimacy that the small groups afforded, the flexible covenanting that they themselves developed, and the shared focus on their prayer life was of extraordinary importance.

The optional silent retreats were attended by about 20 percent of the class each year. I believe that more students would have attended if we had had funding for room and board. For many of the students, this was the most extended time that they had spent in silence in their lives. Literally all who participated in the retreats expressed how powerfully they were affected by this opportunity to open themselves to God's presence for an extended period of time.

Reflections on the Process of Introducing Centering Prayer

THIS HAS BEEN a long road. It has been blessed by the many students from different races, cultures, and religious traditions. Some students have described themselves as secular humanists; others were from the Quaker tradition. There have been several Catholic lay persons and priests, there have been several spiritual directors, and there have been Jewish students—including one Orthodox Rabbi. We found that opening ourselves in silence to God's presence and movement in our lives provided common ground for us to journey together, although often on differing paths.

I contracted with students whose traditions were removed from many of the texts we were reading to select appropriate texts for their reflection, and they did so. Some of my Unitarian Universalist students would resonate with the transcendentalists. Some of the Jewish students resonated with the Jewish Renewal Movement or the Kaballah. These students offered much insight in our collective reflections, both to highlight the differences among our traditions and to provide glimpses of the common theological ground on which we stand.

Students have largely been very enthusiastic about the course. One student told me, "George, you're really boring sometimes, but my life has been changed by this course." Another student recently wrote to me saying that practicing Centering Prayer has become one of the central supports for her ministry. Many students continue the practice and join or form Centering Prayer support groups. There are also D.Min. and Ph.D. students in the course who, working in locations other than in the parish, plan to introduce Centering Prayer into their institutions and seminaries. As I was preparing this manuscript, one colleague who teaches Clinical Pastoral Education stopped me in the hall and said that students who have taken this course and worked with her have been deeply touched by the course. She also noted that one gift that seems to grow from the Centering Prayer process is that students become more empathic with others as they begin to notice their own internal dialogues and how they may impede openness to the other.

While many of my colleagues have been supportive of the course offerings, hardly any of them attended the ongoing Centering Prayer support group held each week in our small chapel. One colleague whom I was telling about my experiences at the ten-day CO retreat responded, "I'd go crazy if I had to be quiet for that long!" My sense is that these courses are culturally different from much of our collective work at the seminary. As in all cross-cultural endeavors, multilayered dialogue must continue if communication is to deepen. My hope is that this paper will be one way to continue this process.

Over the years, I have come to realize that the challenge implicit in this work is not just for liberal American Protestantism in the twentieth century. A conscious practice and examination of the life of contemplative prayer undermines several hundred years of academic history. Only recently, studying the work of Ken Wilber,[8] have I realized that the devaluation of the inner life is a product of the enlightenment, and what more normative exemplar of the enlightenment than the university? Wilber argues that, as we have moved into modernity, we have collapsed interiority into surfaces. He calls this the flatland of modernity. Thus, the modern university and, by extension, the modern seminary have largely collapsed interiors into the exterior. He develops a four-fold classification of reality, looking at a two-fold split between interiors and exteriors and between individuals and groups. He argues for an all quadrants examination of what it is to be a human being—placing equal emphasis on our interior lives and on our exteriors.

Reintroducing interiority into the academy is thus a profound challenge to modernity itself. It is a call to conversion. It is not a call to move back to the pre-modern, mythic-membership mode of being. The promise of reintroducing a contemplative dimension to formal seminary education is to engage what Fr. Thomas calls full reflective self-consciousness with the grace-filled possibilities of the ripening life of prayer. My hope is that these courses can serve as one ecumenical model for encouraging just such a call to conversion.

---

8. Ken Wilber is an extremely prolific writer. For a good introduction to his current thinking I recommend: Ken Wilber, *The Marriage of Sense and Soul: Integrating Science and Religion* (New York: Random House, 1998).

Please find listed below the books that will be used for the next offering of the course "Prayer as the Heart of Religious Leadership." Let me say a word or two about how I introduce the texts. I encourage us to understand the texts as conversation partners and to approach them as we would another person—with kindness, reflection, and an open heart. I introduce the texts and explain how they have been in conversation with me as I continue my journey. The annotated bibliography that is distributed during the course attempts to convey a similar tone—that of introducing one friend to another.

Louis Dupre and James A. Wiseman eds. *Light From Light: An Anthology of Christian Mysticism.* New York: Paulist Press, 1988.

Thomas Keating. *Invitation to Love: The Way of Christian Contemplation.* New York: Continuum, 1996.

————. *Open Mind, Open Heart: The Contemplative Dimension of the Gospel.* Rockport, Mass.: Element Books, 1991.

Francis Nemeck and Marie Coombs. *The Spiritual Journey: Critical Thresholds and Stages of Adult Spiritual Genesis.* Collegeville, Minn.: Liturgical Press, 1986.

Gustave Reininger, ed. *Centering Prayer in Daily Life and Ministry.* New York: Continuum, 1998.

Richard Rohr and Andreas Ebert. *Discovering the Enneagram: An Ancient Tool for a New Spiritual Journey.* New York: Crossroad, 1991.

Ken Wilber. *The Marriage of Sense and Soul: Integrating Science and Religion.* New York: Random House, 1998.

9 ✸

Forgiving The Unforgivable

M. BASIL PENNINGTON

It was a moment that will be forever etched in my memory: I was in the airport in Wichita, waiting to board my plane when the news was flashed on the TV screens—Sadat had been shot. It was not yet known how seriously he had been injured. When I boarded my plane, I found myself seated next to a man from Kuwait. He was dressed in the traditional garb of his country. We began to speak together very amicably, sharing about the different spiritual practices of our particular traditions. After we had been talking for about a half-hour, I expressed the concern that was gripping my heart: the tragedy about Sadat. My friend's response shocked me: "I thank Allah for wiping that curse from the face of the earth." In my shock, I blurted out: "What about peace?" His response shocked me even more. "Peace is no concern of ours."

Up to that time I had lived with the prejudice that everyone wanted peace. The painful awakening of that moment put a lot of things into a new perspective. My time in East Africa was another such awakening experience.

I judge my weeks in East Africa to have been among the most painful of my life. One nun summed up the situation this way. "I speak of the three 'Ds': draught, darkness, and death.

Draught is bad enough. In some places, it is indeed deadly; in others, it inflicts incalculable sufferings, great and small. The lack of electricity certainly has a profound effect on life. When it becomes difficult to do anything from sunset to sunrise, one senses a great curtailment of life."

But it was the prevalence of death and violence that had the most impact on me. There are long prevailing tribal animosities that the Christian spirit often seems to fail to heal. Added to these is the pandemic plague of AIDS. The sisters working among the people said that 35 percent of the people have it, up to 50 percent in the slums. There is virtually no medical care for the victims. What little medical expertise and supplies that are available are used for malaria and other curable diseases. A very high unemployment rate leads hoards of hopeless AIDS victims to form bands or join guerilla groups which sweep down upon villages, rape the women, steal all the supplies they can find and set fire to what remains. In front of our monastery at Butende, Uganda, there is a solitary grave that remains a gruesome reminder for all the nuns within. A sister named Agnes was once hacked to death as she held off a band that had broken through the convent wall. Her bravery enabled her sisters to escape into the forest.

The monastery of Clarte Dieu in Zaire has been repeatedly taken by bands of brigands. After the last raid, the government caught five of the raiders and wanted—to the horror of the nuns—to hang the men at the gate of the monastery. Two days after I arrived, a guerilla band from the hills in the west swept down on a college, locked 80 students in the dormitories and burned them alive, taking 120 others off as hostages. Two days before I left, an armed band from the north calling itself the Army of the Lord seized a girl's college and took off 157 of the young women to be sex slaves.

Immersed in this horror, I was confronted for the first time with the question: Are some sins unforgivable? Can a woman, a nun, a consecrated virgin, who is raped and left with AIDS and a child in her womb, forgive? Can a father who has been forced to watch his wife and daughters raped and brutalized forgive? Can a mother? When it is allowed to happen again and again? Are there unforgivable sins?

I believe in the power of the Resurrection. The first gift of the Risen Lord was the power of forgiveness and the peace it was to bring. "Peace be with you. Whose sins you shall forgive, they are forgiven them."

The Church has tended to give this moment a hierarchical interpretation. Here was conferred the bishops' and priests' power to forgive in the Sacrament of Reconciliation.

Jesus certainly knew our need to unburden ourselves and to hear the word of forgiveness. Many a psychologist has said to me as a priest that they wished they could speak this authoritative word of divine forgiveness.

There is power in the sacrament: power to believe—"Lord, I believe, help my unbelief"; power to accept forgiveness; power to forgive oneself.

But I believe that a non-hierarchical interpretation of this text is also supremely important. When we forgive, any of us, God forgives. Remember the woman taken in adultery (where was the man?): "Has no one condemned you? Neither will I condemn you. Go in peace." And this plays as well at home and with others. When we truly forgive ourselves, we open the space for divine forgiveness.

When the apostles asked Jesus to teach them how to pray, he responded with a prayer that is a whole school of prayer, a whole school of life. It is awesome. And it is frightening. "Forgive us our trespasses as we forgive those who trespass against us." I have always hastened to add in my heart, "Lord, I forgive everyone as fully as I can."

What would that statement mean if I had been a victim of violent abuse, of rape? Could I really forgive?

Of myself, I am certain I could not. As I smarted under such a humiliation and degradation of my human dignity and watched my life being sucked away by an uncontrollable virus, I would not be able to stand in the place of forgiveness and reconciliation. It would be beyond the human. There are unforgivable sins.

But in the power of the Risen Christ? "I can do all things in him who strengthens me." As long as I retained enough of my humanity to make an act of the will, I could by God's grace cut through all and say: I forgive. This, of course, would not immediately heal all the feelings and emotions stored in my physical and mental memory. Some of this residue might never be healed in life's journey. I would have to cut repeatedly through it with acts of forgiveness. This forgiving would itself begin the process of healing. Meditation, Centering Prayer, would little by little continue the process. Others can receive the healing of my forgiveness only if they are willing to repent and accept forgiveness. The same is true of myself. I have to forgive myself of real and imaginary failures.

Part of my forgiveness of others is to pray for them, pray that they receive the grace to repent and be converted. And even as I do this, my own heart is healed. That beautiful human sentiment of compassion begins to grow within me. If I am able to get some distance from my own horrible pain and grief through such prayer, I can begin to realize that a sinner is the sinner he is because he himself has been sinned against, is himself very much a victim.

The acceptance from Christ of the power to forgive is more important to me than to the person whom I do forgive. It alone opens the way to healing of the self, of the other, and of society.

There are indeed unforgivable sins. It is only by the infinite mercy of a God who went so far as to sacrifice his own Son that we can forgive them and they can be forgiven. The forgiveness that I found among our monks and nuns in East Africa is indeed a powerful witness to the Resurrection and the continuing power of the Risen Christ in our midst.

I had gone to East Africa at the request of my order, the Cistercian Order of Strict Observance, more popularly known as the Trappists, to share Centering Prayer and *lectio* with our hard pressed communities there. They certainly were warmly responsive to what teaching I was privileged to give them and enjoyed the times we spent together at the Center and in shared *lectio*. Once again, I found the very simple presentation of Centering

Prayer closely grounded in the Gospels was readily accepted and understood by people from a very different culture. In my teaching, I usually do touch upon the healing power of Centering Prayer. For these dear brothers and sisters, this was most meaningful and precious. We all need this healing. We all have had many experiences heavily laden with emotions that have lodged in our memories and continued to undermine our freedom and joy. Today, we all live in a frenetic world, linked closely by the media, and constantly absorb all sorts of tensions. If these tensions are not released and disposed of, they will build up until they cause us physical or psychological problems. While those who study these things tell us that we can release some of this tension in sleep and some in routine exercise, all agree that the best way to release this tension and be rid of it is meditation. I personally believe that no one can live a fully healthy life in our world today without some effective form of meditation. This obviously has great significance for our friends in East Africa, and I pray that my sharing with them proves a blessing in this regard as well as many others.

Appendix A※

The Method of Centering Prayer

Thomas Keating

Theological Background

THE GRACE OF Pentecost affirms that the risen Jesus is among us as the glorified Christ. Christ lives in each of us as the Enlightened One, present everywhere and at all times. He is the living Master who continuously sends the Holy Spirit to dwell within us to bear witness to his resurrection by empowering us to experience and manifest the fruits of the Spirit and the Beatitudes both in prayer and action.

Lectio Divina

Lectio divina is the most traditional way of cultivating friendship with Christ. It is a way of listening to the texts of Scripture as if we were in conversation with Christ and he were suggesting the topics of conversation. The daily encounter with Christ and reflection on his word leads beyond mere aquaintanceship to an attitude of friendship, trust, and love. Conversation simplifies and gives way to communing, or as Gregory the Great (sixth century), summarizing the Christian contemplative tradition, put it, "resting in God." This was the classical meaning of contemplative prayer for the first sixteen cenuries.

Contemplative Prayer

CONTEMPLATIVE PRAYER IS the normal development of the grace of baptism and the regular practice of *lectio divina*. We may think of prayer as thoughts or feelings expressed in words. But this is only one expression. Contemplative prayer is the opening of mind and heart—our whole being—to God, the Ultimate Mystery, beyond thoughts, words, and emotions. We open our awareness to God whom we know by faith is within us, closer than breathing, closer than thinking, closer than choosing—closer than consciousness itself. Contemplative prayer is a process of interior purification leading, if we consent, to divine union.

The Method of Centering Prayer

CENTERING PRAYER IS a method designed to facilitate the development of contemplative prayer by preparing our faculties to cooperate with this gift. It is an attempt to present the teaching of earlier time (e.g., *The Cloud of Unknowing*) in an updated form and to put a certain order and regularity into it. It is not meant to replace other kinds of prayer; it simply puts other kinds of prayer into a new and fuller perspective. During the time of prayer we consent to God's presence and action within. At other times our attention moves outward to discover God's presence everywhere.

The Guidelines

I. Choose a sacred word as the symbol of your intention to consent to God's presence and action within.

II. Sitting comfortably and with eyes closed, settle briefly and silently introduce the sacred word as the symbol of your consent to God's presence and action within.

III. When you become aware of thoughts, return ever-so-gently to the sacred word.

IV. At the end of the prayer period, remain in silence with eyes closed for a couple of minutes.

Explanation of the Guidelines

I. "Choose a sacred word as the symbol of your intention to consent to God's presence and action within." (cf. *Open Mind, Open Heart,* chap.5)

1. The sacred word expresses our intention to be in God's presence and to yield to the divine action.

2. The sacred word should be chosen during a brief period of prayer asking the Holy Spirit to inspire us with one that is especially suitable to us.
    a. Examples: *Lord, Jesus, Father, Mother, Mary;* or in other languages: Kyrie, Jesu, Jeshua, Abba, Mater, Maria.
    b. Other possibilities: *Love, Peace, Mercy, Silence, Stillness, Calm, Faith, Trust, Yes;* or in other languages: *Amor, Shalom, Amen.*

3. Having chosen a sacred word, we do not change it during prayer period, for that would be to start thinking again.

4. A simple inward gaze upon God may be more suitable for some persons than the sacred word. In this case, one consents to God's presence and action by turning inwardly to God as if gazing upon him. The same guidelines apply to the sacred gaze as to the sacred word.

II. "Sitting comfortably and with eyes closed, settle briefly and silently introduce the sacred word as the symbol of your consent to God's presence and action within."

1. By "sitting comfortably" is meant relatively comfortably; not so comfortably that we encourage sleep, but sitting comfortably enough to avoid thinking about the discomfort of our bodies during the time of prayer.

2. Whatever sitting position we choose, we keep the back straight.

3. If we fall asleep, we continue the prayer for a few minutes upon awakening if we can spare the time.

4. Praying in this way after a main meal encourages drowsiness. Better to wait an hour at least before Centering Prayer. Praying in this way just before retiring may disturb one's sleep pattern.

5. We close our eyes to let go of what is going on around and within us.

6. We introduce the sacred word inwardly and as gently as laying a feather on a piece of absorbent cotton.

III. "When you become aware of thoughts, return ever-so-gently to the sacred word."

1. "Thoughts" is an umbrella term for every perception including sense perceptions, feelings, images, memories, reflections, and commentaries.

2. Thoughts are a normal part of Centering Prayer.

3. By "returning ever-so-gently to the sacred word," a minimum of effort is indicated. This is the only activity we initiate during the time of Centering Prayer.

4. During the course of our prayer, the sacred word may become vague or even disappear.

IV. "At the end of the prayer period, remain in silence with eyes closed for a couple of minutes."

1. If this prayer is done in a group, the leader may slowly recite the Our Father during the additional two or three minutes, while the others listen.

2. The additional two or three minutes give the psyche time to readjust to the external senses and enable us to bring the atmosphere of silence into daily life.

Some Practical Points

1. The minimum time for this prayer is twenty minutes. Two periods are recommended each day, one first thing in the morning, and one in the afternoon or early evening.

2. The end of the prayer period can be indicated by a timer, provided it does not have an audible tick or loud sound when it goes off.

3. The principle effects of Centering Prayer are experienced in daily life, not in the period of Centering Prayer itself.

4. Physical symptoms:
   a. We may notice slight pains, itches, or twitches in various parts of our body or a generalized reslessness. These are usually due to the untying of emotional knots in the body.
   b. We may also notice heaviness or lightness in the extremities. This is usually do to a deep level of spiritual attentiveness.
   c. In either case, we pay no attention, or we allow the mind to rest briefly in the sensation, and then return to the sacred word.

5. *Lectio divina* provides the conceptual background for the development of Centering Prayer.

6. A support group praying and sharing together once a week helps maintain one's commitment to the prayer.

Extending the Effects of Centering Prayer into Daily Life

1. Practice two periods of Centering Prayer daily.

2. Read Scriptures regularly and study *Open Mind, Open Heart.*

3. Practice one or two of the specific methods for every day, suggested in *Open Mind, Open Heart,* chap. 12.

4. Join a Centering Prayer support group or follow-up program (if available in your area).
   a. It encourages the members of the group to persevere in private.
   b. It provides an opportunity for further input on a regular basis through tapes, readings, and discussion.

Points for Further Development

1. During the prayer period various kinds of thoughts may be distinguished. (cf. *Open Mind, Open Heart,* chap. 6–10):
   a. Ordinary wanderings of the imagination or memory.
   b. Thoughts that give rise to attractions or aversions.
   c. Insights and psychological breakthroughs.
   d. Self-reflections such as "How am I doing?" or, "This peace is just great!"
   e. Thoughts that arise from the unloading of the unconscious.

2. During this prayer we avoid analyzing our experience, harboring expectations, or aiming at some specific goal such as:
   a. Repeating the sacred word continuously.
   b. Having no thoughts.
   c. Making the mind blank.
   d. Feeling peaceful or consoled.
   e. Achieving a spiritual experience.

3. What Centering Prayer is not:

   a. It is not a technique.
   b. It is not a relaxation exercise.
   c. It is not a form of self-hypnosis.
   d. It is not a charismatic gift.
   e. It is not a para-psychological experience.
   f. It is not limited to the "felt" prescence of God.
   g. It is not discursive meditation or affective prayer.

4. What Centering Prayer is:

   a. It is at the same time a relationship with God and a discipline to foster that relationship.
   b. It is an exercise of faith, hope, and love.
   c. It is a movement beyond conversation with Christ to communion.
   d. It habituates us to the language of God which is silence.

©1995 St. Benedict's Monastery

Appendix B⊗

Finding Peace at the Center

M. Basil Pennington

Shalom !—Peace !—Salaam !
Peace be with you!

This was the first greeting of the Risen Lord, and it is the heartfelt need and desire of every human person. It is the great concern of our times. But there can be no peace in this world of ours, no peace among nations, unless there is first peace in our own hearts. Only then can we be instruments of his peace, doing the works of justice and love that lead to peace.

Here we discuss two simple, traditional methods of being to the Lord as the Source of our peace:

- Scriptural prayer or Sacred Reading/Listening
- Contemplative or Centering Prayer.

Take some time every day for one or both of these prayer methods.

Allow God to be to you the source of love, life, peace, and happiness that he wants to be.

Sacred Reading

IT IS WELL to keep the sacred Scriptures enthroned in our home in a place of honor as a real presence of the word in our midst.

1. Take the sacred text with reverence and call upon the Holy Spirit.
2. For five minutes (or longer, if you are so drawn), listen to the Lord speaking to you through the text and respond to him.
3. At the end of the time, choose a word or phrase (perhaps one will have been "given" to you) to take with you, and thank the Lord for being with you and speaking to you.

Centering Prayer

SIT RELAXED AND quiet.

1. Be in faith and love to God who dwells in the center of your being.
2. Take up a love word and let it be gently present, supporting your being to God in faith-filled love.
3. Whenever you become aware of anything else, simply, gently return to the Lord with the use of your prayer word. Let the "Our Father" (or some other prayer) pray itself.

John the Baptist's father, Zechariah, tells us that Jesus came "to guide our feet into the way of peace."

We have but to listen to him in his Word, listen to him in our hearts ?—and we shall find the peace we so long for, the peace that this world of ours so desperately needs. We will find that the peace already dwells in us at the center of our being, for there dwells the Prince of Peace, the source of all peace.

The Way to Peace

HOW DO WE find peace? How do we come to possess inner peace so that we can bring peace to others?

On the night before he died, he who is the way, the truth, and the life, our Lord Jesus, gathered his most intimate friends for a final meal. There he poured out his heart to them, sharing with them the deepest secrets of his love. He told them—and us, "The one who loves me keeps my word." We hold fast to all that he tells us and make it the foundation of our lives: "The just person lives by faith."

"The one who loves me keeps my word and my Father and I come and dwell in that one. . . . My word is not my own, it is the word of the one who sent me. The Advocate, the Holy Spirit, whom the father will send in my name will teach you everything and remind you of all that I have said to you." The Father, Son, and Holy Spirit have come and taken up their abode in us to bring to us their own peace, peace that comes from knowing how much we are loved and cared for by the one who has care of all the world, the Almighty, the all-loving.

The way to a deep inner peace is to be in touch with this inner reality. Too often, our prayer is one of words, thoughts, images, concepts—all things produced by our mind. No wonder we often find prayer tiresome, hardly refreshing. Yet, Jesus has said, "Come to me all you who labor and are heavily burdened, and I will refresh you." Prayer should be refreshing. We need to learn to listen, to listen with love, to listen in love.

Sacred Reading

EACH DAY WE want to take five minutes to listen to the Lord speaking to us in his inspired word.

- We take our Bible with great reverence, aware of his presence.
- We kiss the Bible and ask the Holy Spirit who inspired the writer and who lives in us to make the word come alive now in us.
- Then, we listen for five minutes. We respond as we are moved.
- If the Lord speaks powerfully to us, simply abide in his word and presence.
- At the end of our five minutes, we thank the Lord.

Isn't it wonderful we can have him speak to us whenever we want! And we take away from our encounter a thought or word to carry with us through the day.

A Deeper Listening

AT THAT SAME last supper, Jesus told his disciples—all of us, "I no longer call you servants, but friends, because I make known to you all that the Father has made known to me—all the secrets of my heart."

We have been made for a deep intimate friendship with the Lord. Our hearts long for it. As a great sinner who became a great saint once cried: "Our hearts are made for you, O Lord, and they will not rest until they rest in you!" We are not content with just listening to the Lord's words, no matter how wonderful they are. We want a deeper, more experiential union with him.

It is like any true friendship: as it grows, it needs to go beyond words and doing things together and for each other. The image God himself has frequently used is that of the marital embrace, that total being to each other. We need those times of prayer when we listen not just with our ears, our eyes, our minds, but more . . . with our hearts, with our whole being.

This kind of prayer has sometimes been called contemplative prayer or prayer of the heart. It is a prayer of being. The tradition has passed down to us a simple way of entering into this kind of prayer.

This traditional way is today called Centering Prayer.

Contributors ❋

CYNTHIA BOURGEAULT is an Episcopalian priest who has taught at Swarthmore College and the University of Maine at August and was Adjunct Professor of Christian Spirituality at the Bangor Theological Seminary. She organizes and leads workshops, retreats, and courses on Centering Prayer and the Christian contemplative tradition. Her articles have appeared in *Gnosis, Parabola,* and *Benedictine Studies.*

GEORGE F. CAIRNS is assistant professor of Spirituality and Practical Theology at the Chicago Theological Seminary where he teaches courses on spirituality, developing small Christian communities, and engaging structural evil. He is an ordained United Church of Christ Minister who has incorporated Centering Prayer into a street ministry and with prisoners. He presently serves as a coordinator for Contemplative Outreach.

THOMAS KEATING, OCSO, entered the Cistercian Order in 1944. He was appointed Superior of St. Benedict's Monastery in Snowmass, Colorado, in 1958, and was elected Abbot of St. Joseph's Abbey in Spencer, Massachusetts, in 1961. He returned to Snowmass after retiring in 1981, where he established a program of intensive retreats in the practice of Centering Prayer. He is a founder of the Centering Prayer movement and of Contemplative Outreach. He is a former chairman of Monastic Interreligious Dialogue, which sponsors exchanges between monks and nuns of the world's religions; a member of the International Committee for Peace Council, which fosters dialogue and cooperation among world religions; and a founder of the Snowmass Interreligious Conference, a group of teachers from world religions who meet annually to share their experience of the spiritual journey in their respective traditions. He is author of *Finding Grace at the Center, Crisis of Faith, The Mystery of Christ, Awakenings, Invitation to Love, The Kingdom of God, Intimacy with God,* and *Open Mind, Open Heart,* as well as several audio and visual cassettes.

ERNEST E. LARKIN, OCarm, now retired from his teaching of spirituality at the Catholic University of America in Washington, D.C., is active in writing, teaching, and retreat work at the Kino Institute in Phoenix, Arizona.

KAY LINDAHL is the founder of the Alliance for Spiritual Community, a grass-roots interfaith organization which focuses on the dialogue process, and the Listening Center, which offers classes, consulting, and coaching in the sacred art of listening. She also leads workshops on Centering Prayer. A member of the Board of Directors of the North American Interfaith Network and the Mastery Foundation, she is also a representative to the Southern California Ecumenical Council. Kay is a regional coordinator for the United Religions Initiative, a global movement to create peace among religions. A founding member of Faith Episcopal Church, she serves on the Commission on Lay Ministry Development and the Program Group on Missions for the Episcopal Diocese of Los Angeles.

M. BASIL PENNINGTON, OCSO, is a scholar, author, journalist, and a monk of St. Joseph's Abbey in Spencer, Massachusetts. He is one of the monks who distilled and first taught the contemporary form of ancient Christian contemplative prayer, now called Centering Prayer. He is a founder of Cistercian Studies, an institute and publisher of medieval studies. He also is a founder of the Mastery Foundation, which offers Centering Prayer and other support to those in active ministry. Fr. Basil received graduate degrees in Rome in theology and canon law. He has traveled the world as a scholar of monasticism and as a Cistercian superior. Most recently, he has resided at Our Lady of Joy Monastery in Hong Kong, helping to renew the ministry of the Trappist order in China. He is author of countless articles and over fifty books. Included among his numerous books are *Centering Prayer; Centered Living; Daily We Touch Him; In Peter's Footsteps; Breaking Bread; Challenges in Prayer; The Manual of Life; On Retreat with Thomas Merton;* and *Thomas Merton, Brother Monk.*

GUSTAVE REININGER was instrumental in disseminating Thomas Keating's teaching methods in Centering Prayer beyond the monastic community to those in active life. He is a founder and for many years a trustee of Contemplative Outreach, an ecumenical network that teaches Centering Prayer in churches, schools, and places of work. He teaches Centering Prayer and conducts retreats throughout the country. A graduate of the University of Chicago and a former investment banker, he now is a producer and writer of feature films and network television.

EUGENE TAYLOR SUTTON is an Episcopal priest and Associate Rector of St. Columba's Episcopal Church of Washington, D.C. He is the coordinator of Contemplative Outreach activities in metropolitan Washington and teaches Centering Prayer and conducts retreats nationally. Fr. Sutton has taught at Vanderbilt University and is a doctoral candidate at Princeton Theological Seminary.

LYLA YASTION is a doctoral candidate in Anthropology at The City University of New York, studying Centering Prayer groups and Contemplative Outreach as contemporary communities. She has extensive experience in Centering Prayer and has studied world religions, particularly those of the East. She serves on the faculty of College of New Rochelle, New York. She is married, the mother of two sons, and lives in New York City.